Acknowledgements

I would like to thank my wife Digna, for her unfaltering support and for believing in me, even in times where I doubted myself. My beautiful wife was the true force behind making this book a reality. She was always by my side every step of the way pushing and motivating me. Her unconditional love is what catapulted me into doing things that I would have only imagined...and writing this book was one of those things.

I would also like to thank my mother Orquidea, for constantly letting me know that I could accomplish great things and encouraged me to move forward. My mother has always believed in me and also provided me with unconditional love. She has always been present when I've needed her and has given me the encouragement to believe in myself and to never look back at what was, but rather look forward at what can be. This she did despite the headaches I gave her and sometimes still do. She has always sacrificed her own livelihood to give me an opportunity of a better future.

This book is dedicated to the two wonderful ladies in my life whom without, this book would not have been possible. - Laz

U.S. Copyright © 2014

Color Version

ISBN-13: 978-1499745221

ISBN-10: 1499745222

Introduction

I'm sure some of you are somewhat perplexed and asking *"Laz, why are you writing a book on IP's when so many books and websites exist on the subject?"* Well, the answer is simple, I want to get rid of any web of confusion you may have on this particular subject.

IP's have been explained in so many ways that it would take me hundreds of chapters to try and unravel that which has been so unnecessarily raveled…and I'm not about to go through all that work, mainly because I don't want to.

So, after much thought, I decided to put it down in plain text and explain my method, which is the simplest and easiest method available. *"But why Laz?"* you might ask. Well, I wanted you to understand…wait! Let me rephrase that…*"I needed you to understand"* everything that has to do with IP's. After all, they don't call me *"The IP Master"* for nothing.

Hopefully, this book will be the one that will finally fill in all those missing gaps you may have about this much misunderstood subject. However, if this is the first time you read a book on IP's, then you should be pre-warned; you should expect to gain great understanding and a strong foundation of the IP protocol when you read this book; *both on IPv4 and IPv6*. So, if this is what you are hoping to achieve, I believe you have come to the right place.

My IP book will not only help you with the IP part of your Cisco certification, but it will also help you in passing any test you may take in dealing with this subject matter. At the very least, it will let you impress your boss or co-workers when you start subnetting in your head…or fingers. Yes! This book will let you do just that. □

INTRODUCTION

I've been told that besides *"Networking"* many other fields within the scope of IT and Technology need to deal with IP's as well. My sincere goal is for you to carry the knowledge you will have learned here and have the ability to transfer it onto your current or future work environment; making you a greater asset to any institution and/or corporation.

Like I mentioned before, this book is written in a very simplistic and easy to understand manner *(You will NOT find any IP book in the market today that is easier, straightforward, more clear-cut and precise than this one!)*. I call the process of understanding IP's *"Journeys"*, since in my view, this is an adventurous trek to finally reach full comprehension and demystify the whole concept surrounding IP's.

Our first journey will begin with the basics of IPv4. Then, we will work our way into addressing end-devices, switches & routers. From there, we will maneuver our way slowly into the subnetting of an IP Address; *both class-full and class-less*. This book will then take you into the summarization part of IPv4; explaining the importance of it and of course, how to summarize networks.

We will then round off IPv4 with wildcard masking; which you normally use in configuring OSPF, NAT and of course, your access-list.

If you're thinking *"Laz, it's just too much information man!"* don't worry, I have your back on this one ;) In this book I will explain all these topics thoroughly. I will break it down for you in a way that you will have no choice than to understand and comprehend the material. So, expect to see plenty of illustrations and practices within. This, I have done, so you can gain a full understanding of the subject as discussed herein.

Once we are done with the IPv4 portion of the book, we will dive into the now infamous IPv6 protocol...*yes, finally...what we've all been waiting for!!!* This, to me, is extremely exiting…I feel like a kid contemplating my favorite candy! By now you're probably shacking your head aren't you? But I assure you that you will learn its terminology, its format, the diverse sections of it, and learn about the different types of addresses that exist within IPv6 and the benefits that it brings to the world. And yes…how can we forget about the transition mechanisms that this protocol has to offer as well?

The way I see it, no matter how bad we may want to desperately transition to IPv6 (*at least I do*); we will still be dealing with IPv4 and will continue to do so for quite a while into the future. So, there is no going around it guys and gals, we cannot cut corners here.

We have to learn how to configure both protocols so they can work and co-exist with each other for some time to come. So, don't hold your breath for IPv4 to go away any time soon.

Now tell me…are you as excited as I am? This is truly my favorite subject and I hope it comes across in this book.

But let's move on (*I tend to digress a bit, and you'll find this out throughout the book.*); once you acquire a good understanding of the terminology and how to identify a proper IPv6 address, we will finally get to the fun part of SUBNETTING! *"Doc you are insane!"…Nope!* I assure you that you will be subnetting in IPv6 and you will not be using any complicated formulas or any type of physics to do it.

Those of you that know me, should know by now that it is not for me, and I believe or hope, that it's not for you either; otherwise, why get this book?

Let me start by confessing something…I don't like math and never have, and no one is going to convince me that the complicated formulas that are currently used are easier than the method I'm about to show you in this book.

Now, if you DO like math and love to work with formulas, then knock yourself out. Easy is not for everyone you know. But for those like myself, that are always looking to reach the correct answer in the fastest and simplest of forms, then this is the book for you.

Yes, we all know that a calculator is faster and you don't have to think…but in a testing environment, you are NOT allowed to use one. Please, take my word for it. You will be removed from a testing site if you try to take a calculator…trust me on this. I have perfected this method so that I can make life easier for you.

This is the only method where you will be able to do any IP addressing and subnetting in your head and therefore have a greater chance to pass your CCNA certification exam. After all, that is the goal isn't it?

You should know by now that by the time you finish this book, you will be doing IP addressing in your head; and I repeat…without a calculator! After all, this is mainly intended to take a certification exam. Once you get your certification and/or pass your exam, then using a calculator won't be an issue. Go right ahead…use a calculator all day long; in fact, I encourage you to use a calculator to verify what you will have learned here.

Always remember to *"trust but verify"*. After all, you did purchase this book for a reason didn't you?

More than likely you need this information to be able to pass a certification, test or exam or maybe you just feel the need to impress your boss or you need this information to be able to answer any IP questions they may ask when going to a job interview.

You certainly didn't get this book because you had time to spare and wanted to donate money to a good cause...because if you did...I THANK YOU!

For those that are still in doubt and think that you can take a calculator to a testing site, I dare you to walk in to a Pearson Vu center with calculator in hand. See how far you'll get. I'm here to tell you that this book will give you the confidence to answer any questions on IP's by counting with your fingers...or toes for that matter...oh wait!...that's only for IPv4 (*sorry for that*). It's a slightly different story when it comes to IPv6. There, you will definitely need pen & paper, after all it is a 128 bit address.

WOW! We went from 32 to 128 bit address; that was quite a drastic jump wasn't it, but a much needed one at that. Who would have thought that we would now have smart refrigerators that would need an IP address? Technology is great and I love it!

Finally we will have some fun with Hex conversions...did I say FUN? *Yes I did*! It's just a *"good to know"* topic; but seriously, we do need to get comfortable working with Hex numbers since IPv6 is all in hex. Hold on now...don't start pulling your hair out yet, this, of course, is for those unlike myself that have hair, because I will teach you how to use the same concepts we use in IPv4 and transfer it to the new IPv6 protocol.

This is the future guys & gals, and it is here to stay, so we might as well get comfortable with it.

With all this said; sit back, relax and get ready to begin a journey into IP's. It will be a grand adventure in learning and an exciting one as well...Yes! I said *"exciting"* because learning should be all those things; *FUN, EXCITING* and *MEMORABLE!* Why memorable? Well, some stuff you will have to commit to memory, just like you did when you had to memorize the alphabet or your time tables. It's been said *"If it was easy, then everyone would do it"*.

Another reason why I also call it memorable, is because once you see for yourself how easy it is, you will never forget it and think back and laugh at the times that you thought you would not be able to understand IP's….silly you. ☺

However, beware! Because, once you've reached the end of this journey, you will have found true enlightenment on this subject. The information I will give you here is one that you will carry with you for the rest of your life (*if anything, just try NOT to lose this book and carry it with you for the rest of your life!*). It will also be a transformational experience. Because, from this time forward you will look at IP's in a different light and will wonder *"how in the world did I survive without this knowledge? Why would anyone explain this in any other way?* And finally, *"why would anyone try to sabotage my understanding of IP's?"* By the end of this book, IP's will become second nature to you. The fear you had when dealing with IP's will evaporate into thin air and you will no longer have any doubts about tackling an IP related problem. It will be just like riding a bike! (*This of course is meant for those of you that know how to ride a bike – I myself learnt at the age of 15. Hey…it's better late than never*). □

But enough said! I truly hope you enjoy these journeys *"since there will be more than one"* as much as I will enjoy being your guide.

-   *Laz*

Journeys

IP BOOK

IPv4

Terminology

When we speak of the IP protocol, we usually hear words like *"TCP/IP model"*; which we should know by now is the four layer model developed by the Department of Defense *(DoD)* to ensure that there's communication between source and destination, *"wherever that maybe"*, would always be possible, even if WW3 where to happen!

Within this model there are certain terms or words which we need to be familiarized with; words such as *Telnet, SSH, FTP, TFTP, SNMP, HTTP, HTTPS, NTP, DNS, DHCP/BootP* and so on. These are some of the most common *"Protocols"* we should know right off the top of our heads. We need to know what they are used for and the port numbers they use to send information back & forth.

This book is solely dedicated to the understanding of the Internet Protocol *(IP)*, which sits on the TCP/IP model's Internet layer. This is where all the other protocols also exist! They were all created for the sole purpose of supporting this very important protocol…*hint-hint, the one this book is about.* Without the IP protocol, communication would set us back to the dark ages…thank goodness for technology. *Welcome to the 21st century Ladies and Gentlemen!*

Today's devices have what we call software or logical addresses *(The words are used interchangeably)*. We normally call this what?…that's right!, an ***"IP address"***. These addresses, in conjunction with either static or dynamic routing, help create the pathways to the destinations we are trying to get to. We are then able to see these pathways in our routers through our routing tables.

In the IPv4 world, the IP address is broken up into two parts; the network side and the host side. What determines how these two parts are divided is something called *"the subnet mask"*. The subnet mask is the KEY to answering all your questions when it comes to IPv4…but I digress. By the way, I love analogies! So excuse me if I use some of them in this book. I only do it to give you a better understanding and/or to help you visualize the problem we are tackling. So, let's make this analogy for example; one part of the address, *"the network side",* is where you live or reside, this is like your neighborhood. The other part of the address, the host side, is just like your actual house address or *"host address"*…EUREKA...this is you!. This is the part that defines who you are in a particular network (*or neighborhood if you will*). But keep in mind that in reality, it is the subnet mask, NOT the *"Class of Address"*, that defines which network you belong to and who you are within that network.

Now before we go any further, I have reached the point where I have no choice but to show you a figure of the IP header. This is to give you a visual picture of what the IP protocol has to go through every time someone sends a message to a certain destination. But I am not going to get jiggy with it since what I'm striving for is simply for you to visualize it and be somewhat familiar with it, if and when it ever comes up in an exam. Let's just hope it doesn't. But you will be prepared if it does ☺. There's a quote that I love that says more or less the following: *"it is better to be prepared if a situation arises, then for a situation to arise and not be prepared".* Food for thought!

The diagram below is what an IP header carries with it going across a network.

Version (4)	Header Length (4)	Priority and type of Service (8)	Total length (16)	
Identification (16)		Flags (3)	Fragmented offset (13)	
Time to live (8)		Protocol (8)	Header checksum (16)	
Source IP address (32)				
Destination IP address (32)				
Options (0 or 32 if any)				
Data (varies if any)				

Well, here you go! I am NO *"da Vinci"*. But hey,…close enough for government work.

One important protocol that uses IP's; for the sole purpose of letting us know if there are problems on the network, is the *"Internet Control Message Protocol"* or (ICMP). We use it on a daily basis when we ping and we get *"Destination Unreachable"* or *"Request Timeout"*. ICMP is basically a management/messaging protocol that provides hosts with information about network problems and are encapsulated within an IP datagram.

With the awakening of the IPv6 protocol, ICMP has been revamped, to include a lot more features, such as; *Neighbor Acknowledgement, Neighbor Solicitation, Router Acknowledgement* and *Router Solicitation* as well as *Neighbor Discovery*.

Another trouble shooting command that we use on a daily basis that also uses IP's is TRACERT on Windows or TRACEROUTE on the routers. These commands will go through the pathway, whether created statically or dynamically, and lets us know where a problem is occurring.

The last thing I'm going to talk about within the terminology section is about the Address Resolution Protocol (ARP).

In IPv4, ARP finds the hardware address of a known IP address. *How does that happen?* you might ask. Well, it sends out an ARP broadcast. When a request is made looking for a destination host, it is basically saying *"Hey! Who is the owner of this IP address?"* That particular machine replies with its hardware address or its MAC address in order to complete the frame and *voila!* That's when communication takes place. Are you exited yet?

IMPORTANT! ARP only happens in Ethernet segments. Let's look at the following illustration as an example of ARP.

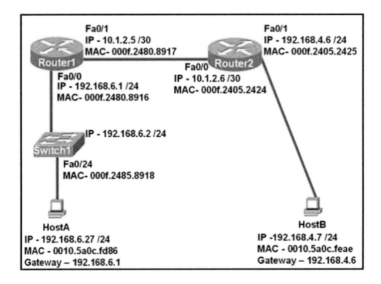

If host A would ping host B for the first time, an ARP request would go from Host A to R1's F0/0 interface to learn the MAC address of that interface. Once you have the MAC address of the F0/0 interface of the router, the packet will then be able to get to R1 from host A. At that time R1 would discard any layer 2 information, query its routing table and make a routing decision based on that routing table on where to send that packet to. Since R1 and R2 are connected using Ethernet, another ARP needs to occur.

R1 would send an ARP request to R2 to acquire the f0/0 MAC address and once it does it can then send the frame. The same process happens on R2 trying to get to host B. The router must know the MAC of the PC in order to complete the packet and be able to send the data to it.

Lucky for us that in IPv6, there is no longer a need for ARP broadcast, because we now have neighbor discovery using link local addresses. *But I'm digressing again.* We will get there soon enough.

IPv4 Hierarchical Addressing

An IPv4 address is a 32 bit dotted decimal address. It is divided into 4 separate sections called "Octets" and they are separated by a decimal. Why these sections are called octets? Let's go back to the basics shall we? Remember that it takes 8 bits to create a byte; therefore, 8 bits X 4 octets would equals a 32 bit address in IPv4.

Below are examples of what an IPv4 address looks like in its different formats.

Decimal: **192.168.1.1**

Binary: **11000000. 10101000.00000001.00000001**

(zero's to the left are ALWAYS omitted)

Hex: **C0: A8:01:01**

(Don't Panic! You will NOT be asked to convert to hex format on the CCNA certification exam)

The reason why an **IP** address is called *Hierarchical* or *Structured* is due to the fact that instead of looking at the entire 32 bit address as a unique identifier of an individual host; the address is broken down into networks, subnet-work addresses and host addresses. You could also consider the broadcast address as another part of the address.

If we were to have an address scheme where the entire address would be the "*Unique Identifier*" of a host, then the router would need to have each and every address that exists in their routing table. That would certainly not be feasible, and in turn, routing would literally be impossible. ☹ …this is a NO-NO!

Network Address

Let's move on to the topic of the "*Network Address*". This identifies the neighborhood you live in (*I'm saying this for visualization purposes only*). When we create "networks", each network obviously has nodes (*the devices connected directly into the network*). All those nodes share that same network address. This is so they can know what neighborhood they reside in. Below, I will give you an example.

Example: **192.168.1.0 255.255.255.0**

This particular address, because of its SUBNET MASK, will have all hosts residing in the **192.168.1.0** network. If however, the SUBNET MASK would change, let us say… to a **255.255.255.248**, then the network would be **192.168.1.16** (*this of course, if it is <u>NOT </u>using the "zero network"- don't worry, this will be explained later ☺*).

Remember that an IPv4 address has two parts; the "*network*" portion and the "*host*" portion. Again, let's use the address above as an example; **192.168.1.100 255.255.255.0**. The first 3 Octets of the address 192.168.1 is the network portion; the .100 would be the host portion. This would then identify that unique individual host on the network.

192.168.1	100
Network Portion	*Host Portion*

IPv4 Address Classes & Types

Classes of Address

Oh boy! Here we go… the topic that just about everyone gets into a freaking frenzy when I mention it. For some odd reason, every time I discuss the *"Classes"* of IP addresses, the hordes get into an insane warpath and want my head on a platter (*and not a silver one at that*). *"There are no such things as classes anymore Laz!"* they hurl at me, as if they could, if they had spears, attempt to penetrate by very being. *Sorry for that Spartacus moment guys and gals, but I get carried away sometimes.*

Going to what I was saying earlier, *"I'm really sorry that I have to prove wrong those that are incredulous that I would dare talk about classes."* I am sorry to disappoint many of you, but you do need to know about "classes" of IP addresses up until the time comes when we will no longer use IPv4. However, that time has not yet arrived! Therefore, my job and responsibility is to explain to you what and how the classes of addresses work and why.

Once we can fully implement IPv6 though, that's when things will take on a different twist. But until such a time arrives, we will have to know the classes of addresses and what they look like. So, without further ado, here we go…..

The classes of address are as follows: Class **"A"**, **"B"**, **"C"**, **"D"** and **"E"**. Each one of these classes has their own specific range, this is to include a default mask and a default number of host. Let's first create a table to best identify the classes and be able to explain each one in detail.

(Note that I did not subtract 2 on the host side)

Class of Address	The Range	Default Mask	Default Number of Host
A	1 – 126	255.0.0.0	16,777,216
B	128 – 191	255.255.0.0	65,536
C	192 – 223	255.255.255.0	256
D	224 – 239	N/A	N/A
E	240 – 255	N/A	N/A

Before we begin explaining the particulars of each class of address, let's get familiarized with the format of an IPv4 address; meaning, how an octet is comprised. Yes, yes…I know I mentioned this before, but I'm going to do it again in a more visual content so as to engrave it in your brain. And by the way, repetition breeds retention, so it certainly won't hurt.

128 64 32 16 8 4 2 1   128 64 32 16 8 4 2 1   128 64 32 16 8 4 2 1   128 64 32 16 8 4 2 1

1st Octet ⬤ 2nd Octet ⬤ 3rd Octet ⬤ 4th Octet

As you already know, each octet has **8** bits with the values of each bit remaining the same in each octet. This means that when we add the bit values together within their octets, they equal a maximum of **255**.

The bit values for each octet are added from left to right to acquire your subnet mask. This format does not change as you can see from the figure above, and it will always remain the same for IPv4. I bet you thought it was going to be harder than this didn't you?

I do, however, want to emphasize that you can also determine the classes of addresses by just looking at the first octet of that address.

Below are some examples:

10.1.0.100	Class "**A**"
172.31.25.90	Class "**B**"
192.168.10.100	Class "**C**"

Moving on, let's begin to start breaking down the classes of addresses.

Let's first discuss the Class "**A**" address using the following table:

Class of Address	The Range	Default Mask	Default Number of Host
A	1 – 126	255.0.0.0	16,777,216
B	128 – 191	255.255.0.0	65,536
C	192 – 223	255.255.255.0	256
D	224 – 239	N/A	N/A
E	240 – 255	N/A	N/A

Go ahead and take a look at the "*range*" column above. You can see that it starts with **1** and goes all the way to **126**. Well then…what happened to the zero? The zero is a unique address and it's already allotted for something else…it is a reserved address.

Hence, we are not allowed to use it; that is why we start with the number **1** *(does that make sense?)*. If you look at the next column, which shows the default mask, you should notice that in the first octet the bits are all **ones** and the rest are all **zero's**. Meaning, you can *NOT* mess with the first octet. Therefore, you will be doing all of your subnetting and/or addressing within any of the other octets. Finally, in the last column, you can see how many host you could have with a class "**A**" address using the default mask. You're probably saying "*WOW, that's a lot of addresses Laz*". Oh yes, I almost forgot…I can't stress this enough! You always, always, always MUST subtract 2 from the host address to get the *USUABLE* addresses. Again, why do we subtract 2? Remember that one address is your network address and the other is your broadcast address. This means that the actual number of addresses would be **16,777,214**. You're probably asking yourself "*Laz man, do we need to remember this?* The answer is a simple *YES!* Why? Because you are in IT ladies and gentlemen and this is the minimal of the basic information that you need to know.

This is precisely why I wrote this book. I wanted to make sure this information stuck and was embedded in your brain. I don't care how many times I repeat myself over and over again, which you will see I do a lot here, as long as I get this point across. If you're thinking "*Laz must be OCD*", I assure you ladies and gentlemen, I am not, although some may argue that point.

Let's now move on to a Class "B" address:

In the second row, *again referring to the table above*, let's look at the class "**B**" address and analyze it. If you look at the second column of the class "**B**" address, you will notice that the range starts with **128**. *Say what? How is that possible? What happened to 127 Laz?* Well, it's very simple, the **127**, which includes the entire range from **127.0.0.0 – 127.255.255.255,** has been reserved for loopback. The loopback is what we use to check and see if our TCP/IP stack is working correctly. The exact address we use would be **127.0.0.1,** again, remember that this is for testing purposes only (*never deviate from the main goal...which is passing your certification exam!*).

We finish off the range in a Class B address with **191**...great! No worries here. Let's move on to the next column and there we see the default mask, which is **255.255.0.0.** Again, the first two octets are completely "*on*" and the last two octets are completely "*off*". This is to enable you to subnet or do your addressing for *nodes* on the network.

Moving on to the last column, we see that we have **65,536** addresses, but wait!...do not forget to subtract 2. By now you should know that this is for the *network address* and the *broadcast address*. We are then left with what?...you got this! The usable addresses of **65,534**. See how things are starting to come together?

Let's move on to the next address on the list...the Class "C" address:

The class "**C**" address is one that we should all be very familiar with and it begins with **192**. There's nothing mysterious or special in this range since it continues on from the last number of **191** all the way to **223**. When you look at the mask for the class "**C**" address, you can observe that the first three octets are all "*on*" and the last octet is "*off*" (example: **255.255.255.0)**, once again leaving only the last octet for you to do your subnetting and/or addressing. With this particular class of address you can have **256** addresses as you can see in the last column on the table above. But, please remember that you must subtract 2 from the host side, which is the *network address* and *broadcast address*.

Consequently, this will leave you with only **254** usable addresses for subnetting and addressing.

We've now come to the last two classes of addresses…"D" & "E".

You really shouldn't concern yourself with these two types of addresses too much, just know about their ranges, just in case they may ask you this in an interview. We really don't do much with these addresses and to tell you the truth, it's not part of your certification exam. But for informational purposes, just know that they do exist and that the class "**D**" address is used for *multicasting* and that the routing protocols use it to send their updates to neighboring routers. The class "**E**" address, however, is just for experimental purposes. ??? Don't ask me why…I did not participate in the decision process. I guess this is something reserved for use in area 51. As a result, I stress to you to please don't concern yourself too much about these two class of addresses. No one really talks much about them…no, actually, they NEVER talk about them. Subsequently, just know their ranges, but that's about it. After all, who cares the why, where and what they are used for? It's nice to know about them, but it's not what will get you certified. Well, there you have it! The classes of addresses; their ranges, their default mask and their default hosts.

Private Addressing

Now that you have familiarized yourself with the classes and ranges of addresses as well as their mask, let's take a look at a special range of addresses called "Private Addresses". These are not routable on the public internet; they are exclusively used for internal purposes within an organization. As usual, let's look at our table below and then we will define each column.

Class	Range	Default Mask	Cisco's Mask
A	10.0.0.0 – 10.255.255.255	255.0.0.0	255.0.0.0
B	172.16.0.0 – 172.31.255.255	255.255.0.0	255.240.0.0
C	192.168.0.0 – 192.168.255.255	255.255.255.0	255.255.0.0

In the class "A" the entire ten (10) range is dedicated to internal addressing. As a result, when you see an address that in the first octet starts with a 10.x.x.x, it will always be an address that is not routable on a public interface. Naturally, you are still left with the last three octets for subnetting and addressing.

In the class "B", it starts to get a bit more interesting; I am referring of course to the first and second octet, whose range is from 172.**16**.x.x – 172.**31**.x.x. *But Laz, why is it **16** to **31** in the 2nd octet?* The majority of networking books will tell you that the subnet mask is as you see it on the column for the default mask, however, the Cisco Press books will explain it to you with a slightly different mask. Let me show you exactly how they came up with the mask of **255.240.0.0.**:

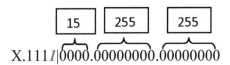

the value to the left of the line, which is highlighted in red is *16*.

Network-ID   Broadcast Address

172.16.0.0   **172.31.255.255**

They start with the actual bit value, and then they add the sum of the other octets according to their particular octet:

15+16 =31, 255+0=255,   and 255+0=255.

This is how Cisco comes up with the mask of 255.240.0.0.

But if you are asked on an exam; *what is the default subnet mask for a class "B" address?*

You will always answer 255.255.0.0.

Now you also know the secret that lies beneath the private class "B" address.

IPv4 Addressing

Classes & Types of Private Addressing

Let's now investigate the class "C" address. This is a very familiar address and it falls under the same criteria as the class "B" address.

If you look at the table again, you will notice that the first two octets do not change; it is only the last two octets that change.

Cisco states that the mask is really **255.255.0.0**. However, I remind you here as well; if asked on an exam, *"what is the default mask for a class "C"?* You will respond; **255.255.255.0**. This is because that is the default mask in TCP/IP.

X.X.00000000.00000000 the first two octets will always be 192.168 in order for it to be a private address.

Network-ID	Broadcast Address
192.168.0.0	**192.168.255.255**

Again, they, I'm referring to *"the powers that be"*, add the sum of the bit values on the right to the corresponding octet in order to get the range.

I'm sure by now you are a bit baffled as to why in the world would I be telling you this. Well, simply put, it was due to the curiosity of many of my students asking how these numbers were chosen. So, I decided to put their minds at ease *…and yours as well*. You can find this information in any Cisco Press book and I'm pretty sure you can Google it too.

The grand finale to this section is just simple definitions of reserved IP addresses that we do NOT use, but DO need to understand their importance on a network.

Loopback: As stated previously, it is used to test the TCP/IP stack. The actual address used is **127.0.0.1**, or you can simply replace the IP with the word "*Loopback*".

Layer 2 Broadcast: This type of broadcast is all in hexadecimal format using all "**F's**", **FF:FF:FF:FF:FF:FF**. These are sent to all nodes in a LAN segment.

Layer 3 Broadcast: This type of broadcast is in decimal format using all **255**'s in the address: **255.255.255.255**. They are sent to all nodes on a network.

Unicast: this particular type of address is a single source that is sent to one destination.

Multicast: These addresses are sent from a single source to many destinations. As stated earlier, your routing protocols use these addresses to send updates to neighbor routers; for example: EIGRP uses the following multicast address **224.0.0.10**.

APIPA: "*Automatic Private IP Address*". These addresses are present only when DHCP is enabled and the host is incapable of receiving an IP address. These addresses are NOT routable.

IPv4 Subnetting

Why Do We Subnet?

Yeah Buddy…here is where the fun really begins!

We need to take this ginormous network we just created and break it up into smaller chunks. *Why?* You might ask.

Well, this is why…we've realized that we can not properly administrate a network of that size. Especially if it's an Ethernet network, which by the way, about 99.9% of the time these networks are Ethernet. Therefore, we have something called CSMA/CD. This is the access method for Ethernet Networks and it is how packets get onto the media to send data across. Not to mention that the layer 2 broadcast will KILL our network. This, on top of the fact, that we would have to deal with the security issues as well.

One network accessing another network, willy-nilly? I don't think so!

It really boils down to eliminating broadcast and noise on your network.

Let me illustrate what I mean with the picture below.

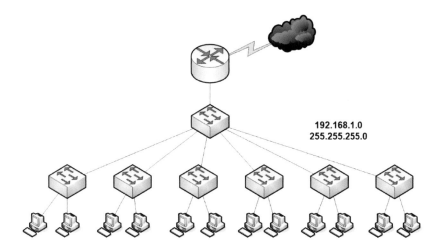

192.168.1.0
255.255.255.0

As you can see in the illustration above, all the PC's are in the same network. This means that every time a node tries to send a packet to any destination, all nodes on the network pay attention to that noise, therefore, slowing down the network.

Let's imagine that the PC's connected to the switches are classrooms, and that those switches in these classrooms are connected to one core switch which in turn connects to the main router that goes out to the internet.

So…let's say that class starts at 9am sharp, and the students are sitting at their desk, with their computers on and are already logged in. But, "EVERYONE IS TRYING TO GET TO FACEBOOK!" However, no one can get to the internet. *What happened?* The network will start crawling right? To top it off, the poor IT guy is also trying to send an image to a couple of computers he did not finish the night before… *AHHH*…the shock! Now the network now goes from a crawl to a complete STOP!. No one will be able to do anything at all. Even a simple task like printing will become utterly impossible.

Why is that Laz? Well, even though we have switches, we are all under one broadcast domain and forced to listen to any noise on the media.

So what do we do?... *ta-ta-ta-da*...SUBNETTING to the rescue! In this scenario, we would separate each switch into its own subnet. This would mean each would have its own broadcast domain. Meaning, it will not hear the noise of the other networks it's trying to reach...to include the IT guy who is trying to image those couple of computers in a specific class room.

Let's illustrate one way we could do this.

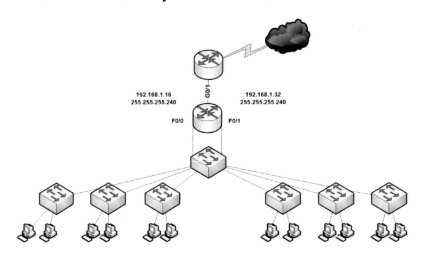

Now, would you agree this is somewhat better? We have increased from one (1) broadcast domain for the LANS to two (2) broadcast domains by subnetting the networks and putting them into different interfaces of the router. When a node on one network attempts to communicate with one computer on that same network, they only hear their own noise... or do they? The other network is oblivious as to what is going on...hmm?. Does this mean that the more broadcast domains we have, the fewer number of nodes exists on that subnet, making the network run more efficiently? You got it! And it also makes sense doesn't it? The fewer people on a segment, the less noise they generate.

Now, by no means is the above illustration the best method of subnetting the network. It would be nice, nonetheless, if each one of those switches would be its own broadcast domain and its own subnet. That way we could increase the amount of broadcast domains even further at layer 2; which would really tweak our network to work more efficiently.

However, the reality is, that even though the core switch is connected to different interfaces on the router, the LAN switches are all connected to the core switch, which still creates one broadcast domain. Consequently, all computers are still forced to listen to noise placed on the media. Tricky-tricky!

To really segment a network, you should do it at layer 2, and you would NEED to use Vlans. That is how each switch can be its own broadcast domain within its own subnet. Thus, a particular network would not hear any of the other networks' noise.

To know which device separates broadcast domains and collision domains is very important. Knowing what functionalities these devices bring into the picture is of equal importance.

IPv4 Subnetting

Why Do We Subnet?

A better topology is called *"a router on a stick"*. I will show how that would look, but we are not going to get jiggy with it here either. We need to know how to subnet so we can assign the networks to each VLAN. Thus, let me illustrate the *"Router on a stick"* method, so we can then begin with subnetting the address.

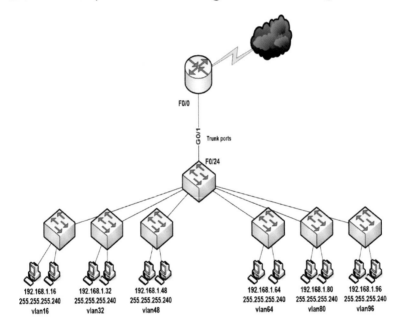

Here, you can see that we have increased to seven (7) broadcast domains due to the VLAN's, and 19 collision domains. This will make a huge difference on the performance of the network. We have also isolated each of the LAN's traffic within itself. Thereby, if you should need to send data to another LAN, it would have to go through the router. No one else will be the wiser.

The purpose of subnetting is to create smaller, more efficient, manageable and secure networks. You would do this at layer 2 by creating multiple Vlans; and since each VLAN has its own subnet, you have now increased the amount of broadcast domains and reduced the amount of broadcast per network.

How Do We Subnet?

Now, you know the "why". But how or where do we begin to subnet an address? There are a million ways to subnet an address. Everyone has their own unique method and you can look at all the different books, or the thousands of YouTube videos or even Google the types of subnetting and you will get tons of information on the different ways and/or variations of subnetting out there. However, I am going to show you one simple method that you can apply using your fingers. No need for calculators and you'll be able to do it in under 30 seconds - MAX! It's taken me years to perfect this method, and so I am writing this book to present this method to you…consider it a gift.

The key, as stated previously, is your subnet mask. If you are given the mask, then that's all you need to focus on. Let's say you are given the following mask **255.255.255.248** and are asked to find how many networks and host can be used with this mask or what is the Network-ID, Range and Broadcast address for the second network? This is quite easy if you use my method of course!

First, let start by focusing on? You got it!...on the last octet of course. That is the octet that is partially on and off. This is where you are going to do all your calculations.

Let's break it down:

128 64 32 16 8 4 2 1

X.X.X.11111|000   THIS IS ALL YOU NEED TO DO, DRAW YOUR LINE

1. How many networks?

   (You count from Left to Right, starting with 2, and double as you go)

   a. **32** Networks

2. How many hosts?

   (You count from Right to Left, starting with 2 and double as you go)

   a. 8-2=6

(Why do we subtract 2? Because we need a NetID and the broadcast address)

Network-ID	Range of Useable addresses	Broadcast Address
X.X.X.8	X.X.X.9 – X.X.X.14	X.X.X.15
X.X.X.16	X.X.X.17-X.X.X.22	X.X.X.23

Can see how easy it is to get the number of host and networks? But how do we come up with network, range and broadcast addresses? Well, if you look at where we drew the line; the bit value to the left of the line will ALWAYS be how your network increments, which in this case is **8**. The bits to the right get added; in this case 4+2+1=7 so you would take that "7", which is your broadcast calculation number and add it to the Network-ID, thereby giving you the broadcast address. You must, however, make sure you are adding the 4th Octet to the 4th Octet. Sometimes a simple error can throw you off.

To clarify it further, I have broken down the design if you will, so you can understand each section from the problem above.

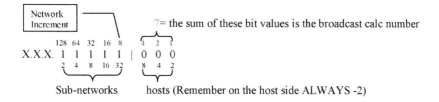

Before we continue with subnetting, I would like to explain something called subnet-zero. This is something that is sometimes asked in the CCNA exam and it has certainly been used in the real world for some time now.

Notice that I did not subtract 2 from the Network side. Subtracting 2 or NOT subtracting 2 depends on the instructions you will be given: either *"use the Zero network"* or *"do not use the Zero network"*. This is the indicator to know when to subtract 2 or when not to subtract 2.

I know you're getting this!

Let us take a look at an easy example:

$$192.168.1.32 \ 255.255.255.224 \ \overset{3231}{\underset{2\ 4\ 8}{x.x.x.111|00000}}$$

Using the Zero Network

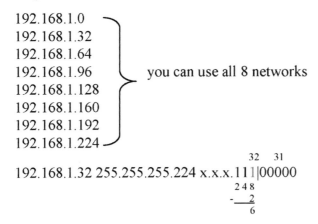

192.168.1.0
192.168.1.32
192.168.1.64
192.168.1.96   you can use all 8 networks
192.168.1.128
192.168.1.160
192.168.1.192
192.168.1.224

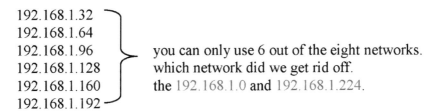

192.168.1.32 255.255.255.224 x.x.x.111|00000

Not using the Zero Network

192.168.1.32
192.168.1.64
192.168.1.96   you can only use 6 out of the eight networks.
192.168.1.128   which network did we get rid off.
192.168.1.160   the 192.168.1.0 and 192.168.1.224.
192.168.1.192

At one point, in a time long forgotten, routers did not understand how to use these two networks. Therefore, we would subtract two from the network side as well. But in today's routers, that is no longer an issue and we are allowed to use all available networks. Life is getting easier as technology advances, does it not? Anyway, I think so!

What makes all this possible is the IOS or *Internetworking Operating System* of the router which has the command - *"IP SUBNET-ZERO"*- **on**, by default.

Why am I throwing this monkey wrench at you, because you will be asked questions on this subject (i.e.: *if using the Zero Network, what would be the subnet?*). Do not take the Zero Network into consideration. This is only so you can recognize what the Zero Network is. I hope this clarified it a bit. If not, just go over this section again and again and you will eventually get it. Remember that I have YouTube videos explaining this subject as well and practice, practice, practice...I cannot stress this enough.

Now, let's re-cap...just to drive it home one more time.

If *"you DO use* the Zero *Network"* - DO <u>NOT</u> SUBRACT 2!

If *"you are NOT using the Zero Network"*, - YOU <u>MUST</u> SUBRACT 2.

End of discussion. GOT IT?

Subnetting a Class "C" Address

Ok, I have drawn out the road map to subnetting, but let's keep practicing with different examples.

Let's go ahead and start using different classes of addresses in different situations.

However, before we go on, I would like to start using CIDR notation instead of Dotted Decimal notation for the subnet mask. It's just too much typing and frankly it's tiresome.

So instead of typing 255.255.255.0 I will use **/24**; they both mean the same thing. The "/" is called the CIDR and the 24 means how many bits are "**on**" from left to right.

Let me give you a guide that you MUST commit to memory:

This table will save your life... trust me on this one!

Bits on	Decimal value
10000000	128
11000000	192
11100000	224
11110000	240
11111000	248
11111100	252
11111110	254
11111111	255

Now that you have memorized the table above, let's now do some commonly asked questions:

1. You have the following Class "C" address: 192.168.1.0/24. You need to subnet this address into six separate networks; what mask would you need?
   a. /26
   b. /27
   c. /24
   d. /30

To attack this problem you first need to figure out what octet you will be working on. In the scenario given, the class of address tells us that we will be working in the last octet. Also, if you look at the CIDR, it's a dead giveaway. Once you figure this out, then all you need to do is count from left to right, starting by two and double as you go, to reach your objective of six networks; at that point you would draw your line.

Let's visualize this:

X.X.X.1 1 1|0 0 0 0 0

2 4 8

In this example, you would need to turn on three bits. *Wait a minute Laz, don't we need six networks?* Yes we do, but here we had to go over the six networks because we had no other alternative. Let's analyze - two bits would have only given us four networks and that was not enough for the requirements needed so we had to go one bit over to get the six networks we want and then some.

Now that we understand that, let's move continue.. Since we now have our line, what is the mask? If you look at the table, three bits on gives us 224. None the less, aren't we looking for the CIDR? The **X's** represent all bits **on**; therefore, 8+8+8+3=27. This means that the only possible answer is a */27* which equates to 255.255.255.224. Easy stuff right? ☺

Are you keeping up?...yes, no, maybe so? *"Laz bro, I think you've left something out!"* Possibly, I know that I may have eluded some important information as to how I converted CIDR notation to a Dotted Decimal notation. And since I don't want to leave you in the dark, here's the explanation that will have your head spinning; are you ready for it?...the secret is that you first need to add the bit values together...THAT's IT! The mystery is over guys and gals. It really doesn't get any simpler than that.

Let's look at the following example:

/20 = X.X.1111|0000.00000000 255.255.240.0

In this example the "**X**" represents **8** bits "**on**". Which means you added the entire bits on that octet together to come up with a value of 255. You would do the same for the 2nd octet. In the third octet, however, you would have to add 128+64+32+16 to get to 240. That is how you would get these values. On the other hand, if you memorize the table I gave you (*you know the one I said would save your life*), you would have no need to add, it would become second nature to you, just like the time tables you memorized in elementary school. I strongly suggest that you MEMORIZE the table I gave you, like if your life depended on it. Finally, the last octet is all zeroes.

2. You have the following IP address 192.168.100.90/29, what sub-network address does the IP address belong to.

    a. 192.168.100.64
    b. 192.168.100.80
    c. 192.168.100.96
    d. 192.168.100.88
    e. 192.168.100.0

Once again, to tackle this question you first need to know in which octet you are going to be focusing on. This question is easy because you are given the subnet mask or CIDR /29. Meaning you are in the last octet. By now we should already know this.

So, let's do another example for visualization purposes:

X.X.X.1 1 1 1 1 | 0 0 0

The bit value highlighted is 8, which is the network increment, therefore we must increment by 8 until we get to 90, which is the number within the fourth octet.

This means that we could increment as follows: 8, 16, 24, 32, 40, 48...and so on. That, however, takes too long! And as you should know by now, I like things simple, short and to the point! But again, I digress...you could ask yourself, "*what number can I multiply by 8 to get close to 90 without going over?"* Well, how about **11x8 = 88**. Hey, that works for me! You certainly can't use **12x8 = 96** - t's just too big and you would go over.

As a result, the sub-network address is **192.168.100.88**. Here, you can even use your multiplication table to help you out.

Let's try another scenario:

In the following topology PC1 cannot communicate with the Web Server.

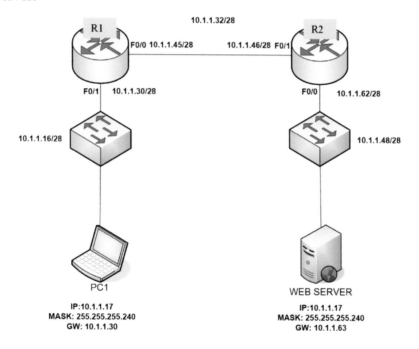

What is the problem?

    a. PC1 has the wrong subnet mask
    b. PC1 has the wrong gateway address
    c. The IP address on R2 F0/1 is invalid
    d. The Web Server is using a wrong IP address for the subnet

e. The Web Server is using an invalid address for a gateway address.

The correct answer is "e" because the gateway address the server is using is a broadcast address, which cannot be assigned to any node, therefore, it is invalid.

Once again, to solve this, we must first locate where the line needs to be drawn. Remember, you have a Dotted Decimal mask of **255.255.255.240** which is the same as CIDR /28.

Hence, you need to break it down as follows:

X.X.X.1 1 1 1 | 0 0 0 0

The bit value that is highlighted is **16**, therefore, you must increment to the highest IP in the network...which is **x.x.x.63**.

Network	Valid Range	Broadcast
10.1.1.16	x.x.x.17 – x.x.x.30	10.1.1.31
10.1.1.32	x.x.x.33 – x.x.x.46	10.1.1.47
10.1.1.48	x.x.x.49 – x.x.x.62	10.1.1.63
10.1.1.64 (Too high)	Not Concerned	Not Concerned

As you can see, it does not matter what scenario you might be presented with, the key is where you draw the line! "*No, I'm not screaming at you*" I just want to emphasize the importance of "**the line**".

Once you are aware that you can answer any question that may be thrown at you by just drawing the line; (i.e.: *what's your increment, how many subnets or hosts do you have, etc.*) then you can easily figure out your subnet mask.

Later on I will show you, using the same diagram, how to come up with the wildcard mask. As we say in the military, *"repetition breeds retention"* so practice until it becomes second nature. I cannot stress this enough!!!

Well, we just learned the concepts of subnetting; which is really just figuring out where to draw the line. And we found out that this, in turn, will give you all the answers you need. Throughout the rest of this book, you might see me referring to this line as, what I like to call, *"the magic line"*.

We should now be very familiar with a class "C" address as in our previous example. In which we were only working with the last octet. If you are still somewhat confuse, just go over the section again until you become a master at it. ☺

Subnetting a Class "B" Address

Now let's spice it a bit and make it a bit more interesting. What happens if you are given a class "B" address instead and would have to work with the last two octets? Let's dive right in and see what happens in this scenario, shall we?

Let us try some of the same commonly asked questions but this time for a class B.

1. You have the following Class "B" network address: 172.31.96.0/19.
   You need to subnet this address into 64 separate networks. What mask would you need?
   - a. /24
   - b. /25
   - c. /22
   - d. /21

43

We would attack this just like we would any other subnetting problem. Where would you focus in drawing the magic line? Well, I already gave you the CIDR, so you should know that your line will be 19 bits in.

Let's work it out:

X.X.1 1 1|0 0 0 0 0 . 0|0 0 0 0 0 0

2 4 8 16 32 64

Here, the original line was at 19 bits **on**... now you have moved the line 6 more bits to the right, which makes it 25 bits **on**, correct? Therefore, the answer is /25 which equals 255.255.255.128.

The reason the value on the last octet is 128, is because that is its bit value.

This is just repeating the same concept isn't it? We just have to make sure we work with both of the last two octets. This is where most people get confused when working with a class "B" address.

Let's continue working with a class "B" address to get a good handle on it.

2. You have the following IP address:
    172.20.156.98/18.

    What subnet does the address belong to?

    a. 172.20.156.0
    b. 172.20.144.0
    c. 172.20.128.0
    d. 172.20.0.0

Now we know the drill don't we?

X.X.1 1 | 0 0 0 0 0 0 . 0 0 0 0 0 0 0 0

The bit value highlighted to the left of the line is 64, which is the network increment. Therefore, your focus should be on the third octet. We would then need to increment by **64** to get close to **156** without going over.

It should look like this: **0, 64, 128, 192**, thus, the answer is 172.20.128.0 subnet.

I know that 192 is larger than 156. *But keep in mind that we are incrementing by 64 on the third octet.*

The following will give you a better visualization of this particular problem:

3. Using the same address above, what is the range and broadcast address?

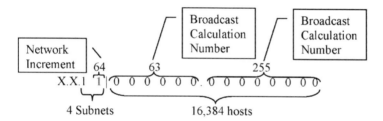

Network ID	Useable range	Broadcast Address
172.20.0.0	172.20.0.1 – 172.20.63.254	172.20.63.255
172.20.64.0	172.20.64.1 – 172.20.127.254	172.20.127.255
172.20.128.0	172.20.128.1– 172.20.191.254	172.20.191.255
172.20.192.0	172.20.193.1– 172.20.255.254	172.20.255.255

Remember, that we can use the exact same concept used for the class "C" address, and apply it to the class "B" address; the only difference in a class "B" address is that you will be working with two octets instead of one.

Subnetting a Class "A" Address

The last address we will talk about, is the class "A" address. It is very rare that you will get a question on subnetting a class "A" address. But, just to cover all the bases in case you are that one lucky individual to get a question on a class "A" address on the exam, I will give you one simple and quick example.

Subnetting a class "A" address is no different than the other classes, you just need to pay attention to **one (1)** more octet.

Let us say you are given and address of 10.16.25.22/12 and are asked to find the subnet, useable range and broadcast address. Again, remember to find the *"magic line"*. Once you've done that, you will have the mask.

Let us begin!

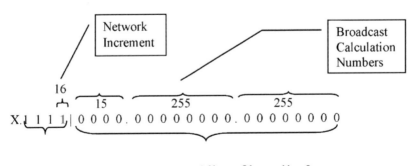

16 Subnets   Allot of hosts!! :-0

Network ID	Useable Range	Broadcast Address
10.0.0.0	10.0.0.1 – 10.15.255.254	10.15.255.255
10.16.0.0	10.16.0.1 – 10.31.255.254	10.31.255.255
10.32.0.0	10.32.0.1 – 10.47.255.254	10.47.255.255
10.48.0.0	10.48.0.1 – 10.63.255.254	10.63.255.255

Well, by now you should know all there is to know about subnetting and that just about everything is easily solved by just finding that *magic line*! You should also be familiar with your network increment, which is the bit value to the left of the line. You should also understand that the sum of the bit values to the right of the line, becomes the broadcast calculation number. Therefore, if you add the broadcast calculation number to the network ID, *in the appropriate octets of course*, then you get your broadcast address. This is a piece of cake!

So to recap…"what is it that you need to master subnetting?" you need to know your bit values, which do not change from octet to octet. How easy is that!

Believe me, once you have mastered this concept, you will become the ***Jedi Master*** of IPv4 subnetting! Of course, practicing over and over again is the ONLY way you will master this concept. This is not something that you will get in just one try. That is why throughout the book, I stress the importance of practicing. I know that it may be tedious or boring at times, but in the long-run, it will pay off.

IPv4 Variable Length Subnet masking

Implementing VLSM

All right now…let's clear our heads, *"you might want to shake it a little to make sure everything falls in the correct slots and remove all the noise out of it – you may also want to step away for a bit to reboot. I do this myself and find it very helpful. I come back with a fresh mind and am able to continue without feeling overwhelmed. I know it's a lot of information to take in, but you guys can handle it"*.

By now, you should have mastered the concepts of subnetting in IPv4. You should know that you need to take a network and cut it up into smaller networks correct? Conversely, if you noticed, they all have the same subnet mask; this is called, class-full subnetting. Obviously, this is not very practical when we are discussing public IP's. We all know by now that the reason we have depleted the public IPv4 addresses, is for the simple reason that no one expected the exponential growth of the internet and its evolution throughout the relatively few years since it's been around…this is truly astonishing isn't it?

In IPv4, corporations would have been assigned public IP's using their default boundaries; so let's elaborate a little bit here; If you were a "company" who had a public presence and needed 2,000 IP's, you would have been assigned a class "B" public address with its default mask of /16. This meant you had 65,534 addresses available to use! Wow…that's quite a bit wouldn't you say? On the other hand, if you were a company in need of 200,000 Public IP's, you would have been assigned a class "A" address with a default mask of /8. Who can tell me how many address are available here? If you said 16,777,214 then you would be correct! You might be looking at this and subconsciously think, *"what a waste of addresses!"* Needless to say we were very wasteful at the beginning of time. But let us not lay blame, let's try and repair the damage or at the very least contain it.

Once it was realized that there were too many addresses being wasted, *"the powers that be"* came up with a plan to try to fix the problem. Their solution came in the form of VLSM or Classless subnetting. This is what came to the rescue and fix the waste…or should I say, slow down the inevitable depletion of IPv4 addresses and buy us more time.

As we know, almost every device needs an IP address; (i.e.: computers, printers, plotters, phones, vehicles, TV's, watches, refrigerators...etc). But IPv4 can only hold 4 billion addresses. If my math is correct, we have over 7 billion people on planet Earth, and most of them have more than one (1) device that uses an IP address. (*I myself have about 20+ devices that require IP addresses*), some might have way more than that, but for argument purposes let's just say that everyone in the planet requires 1 device with an IP address. *4 billion IPv4 addresses for 7 billion+ people?* There's something wrong with that picture…IPv4 was just not going to cut it anymore was it?

Here comes IPv6 to the rescue. This protocol can hold 340 Undecillion addresses (*Yes! that is a real word. You can Google it*). But I digress again since we will talk about IPv6 later in the book.

Ongoing; with the use of VLSM we were able to actually move that preverbal line, we became so familiar with, to adjust the subnet mask to meet the needs of the network as best as possible without having to waste too many addresses in the process. On a side note…other mechanism or attempts to slowdown the depletion of IPv4 addresses was the NAT protocol, specifically NAT Overload (*or PAT as it is also known – you can use the term interchangeably*), which allowed us to use one public address per 65,000+ internal users. I'm just throwing it out there for your own knowledge but also because you will need to know about NAT for your CCNA certification exam, and most definitely in a "*real world*" scenario.

But let's continue; this whole thing started a sort of ripple effect. Once we started using VLSM, our routing protocols also had to be upgraded because RIPv1 and IGRP did not understand the subnet portion of the address. These protocols assumed they all had the same mask in the network; meaning, if you had a class A network that was subnetted, the routing protocol would assume that the default masks was /8 and therefore, packets would get lost. So using masks such as; /30, /28, /25 would create a huge problem; they would not know where to send the data. You might be asking "*Laz, how did they fix the problem?*" *That's a very good question.* RIPv2 and EIGRP came to the rescue this time. These protocols understood the subnet mask portion of the address; although, a very important command *"NO AUTO-SUMMARY"* when configuring RIPv2 or EIGRP must be used when configuring these two routing protocols, if you don't or just don't want to, then you might as well run the older protocols and forget about VLSM altogether. But, I'm digressing again…we will discuss routing protocols in depth in another book; this one is dedicated to IP's only.

So let's get down to the nitty-gritty and see how we can implement a VLSM network. Remember to keep in mind that I will be using private addresses and that VLSM was meant to be used for the depletion of public IPv4 addresses. Confused yet? Don't worry, I got you. , I'm here to unravel the mystery of these protocols and to make sure that at the end you will understand the method to the madness…let the fun begin!

Let's say you are given the network address of **172.20.0.0/16** to work with and you had to design a VLSM network based on the topology below, what is your starting point?

VLSM has rules we need to follow; One (1), start with the highest number of IP's, two (2), always use the next available IP address and three (3), always start from the zero network.

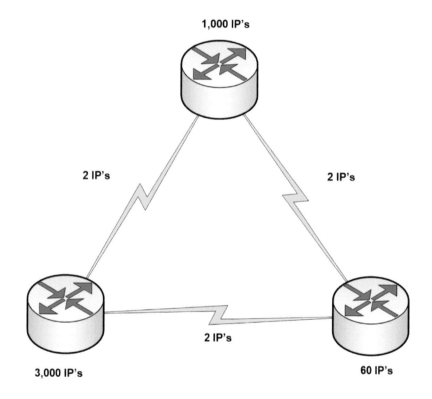

1,000 IP's

2 IP's   2 IP's

2 IP's

3,000 IP's   60 IP's

172	20	1	1	1	1	0	0	0	0	0	0	0	0	0	0	0	0
3000 H		65536	32768	16384	8192	4096	2048	1024	512	256	128	64	32	16	8	4	2

172	20	1	1	1	1	1	1	0	0	0	0	0	0	0	0	0	0
1000 H		65366	32768	16384	8192	4096	2048	1024	512	256	128	64	32	16	8	4	2

172	20	1	1	1	1	1	1	1	1	1	1	0	0	0	0	0	0
60 H		65366	32768	16384	8192	4096	2048	1024	512	256	128	64	32	16	8	4	2

172	20	1	1	1	1	1	1	1	1	1	1	1	1	1	1	0	0
2 H		65366	32768	16384	8192	4096	2048	1024	512	256	128	64	32	16	8	4	2

Number of host	Network ID	Range	Broadcast Address	CIDR
3000	172.20.0.0	x.x.0.1 – x.x.15.254	172.20.15.255	/20
1000	172.20.16.0	x.x.16.1 – x.x.19.254	172.20.19.255	/22
60	172.20.20.0	x.x.20.1 – x.x.20.62	172.20.20.63	/26
2	172.20.20.64	x.x.20.65 – x.x.20.66	172.20.20.67	/30
2	172.20.20.68	x.x.20.69 – x.x.20.70	x.x.23.71	/30
2	172.20.20.72	x.x.20.73 – x.x.20.74	x.x.20.75	/30

As you can see, all we did is start with the highest number of host and work our way down to the lowest number of host; always using the next available IP address for the next Network ID and then adding the broadcast calculation numbers to their perspective octet. Remember also that since the purpose of VLSM is to reduce the waste of public IP addresses, I started using the "Zero Network", meaning I started from the number "*zero*".

If you are going to design a network using VLSM, you must ensure you use a routing protocol that is capable of using VLSM, such as RIPv2, EIGRP or OSPF.

Like I said before, it is really not that difficult, but, you do need to practice, practice and practice again!

Let's analyze the drawings and table below. It is color coded so you can follow along with a visual to make it easier to dissect.

BTW, just so you don't forget what the numbers mean, I have re-draw the diagram for you with their applicable labels as follows:

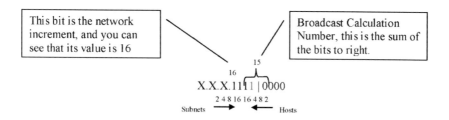

I hope this helped you understand and grasp the idea that I'm trying to convey here. ☺

IPv4 Summarization

Its Purpose & Configurations

Well, you finally got through subnetting and VLSM. Now comes time to Summarize or as Spock would call it, *"Route Aggregation Captain"*. (*You might notice that I'm a big fan of the original Star Trek*). What this really means is, that we must take a bunch of small networks and clump them together into one or maybe two networks, and then we would need to advertise them to our core routers, hence, making their routing tables smaller. There is no need for your core routers to know about all your different LAN's in order to make a routing decision. Another use of *"Route Aggregation"* is to advertise a summary-address. This is to enable a device, at the destination level, to be able to distribute the IP's as it sees fit.

Summarization would allow for lower processing time, when a router analyzes its own routing table to see which path it needs to take to get to a destination.

I think I have mentioned this before, but, in case you missed it, here I go again. Cisco has a standard called the *"Cisco Three Layer Model"* This model, just like the OSI model, is a theoretical model. The model simply informs you which roles certain routers may perform based on where it sits on the topology; let's look at the following:

Cisco's Three Layer Model

Core	The only purpose of the Core layer is to switch information reliably and quickly.
Distribution	The primary purpose of this layer is providing routing, filtering, WAN access and to decide how much data can access the core. This layer can also be called the "Workgroup Layer".
Access	This layer also called the "Desktop Layer" is an extension of the Distribution layer. This layer is where we talk about collision domains and technologies such as Ethernet or Gigabit.

Important to note: *Just because there are three layers, it does not mean you must have three different devices, remember this is a theoretical model.*

With summarization there are some rules that you should follow. The first being that, the network should start with an even number and have an even number of networks as to not waste any IP's in the process; thereby not introducing any IP's in the network that do not need to be there.

The other rule would be in summarization, which is the opposite of subnetting. There is a contrast that can be seen here. In subnetting, we would move the line to the right and get a larger subnet mask and fewer hosts. In summarization however, we move the line to the left and get a smaller subnet mask and a greater number of hosts. This would bring the networks together as one. Keep in mind that these had been separated prior to summarization.

So let's reiterate; the purpose of summarization is to keep the routing tables small so the router does not have to go through a huge list of networks to make a routing decision.

Below is an example of what I mean:

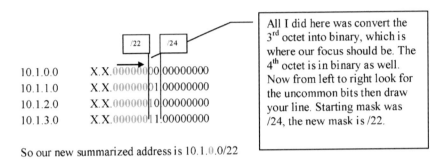

10.1.0.0   X.X.00000000 00000000
10.1.1.0   X.X.00000001 00000000
10.1.2.0   X.X.00000010 00000000
10.1.3.0   X.X.00000011 00000000

All I did here was convert the 3rd octet into binary, which is where our focus should be. The 4th octet is in binary as well. Now from left to right look for the uncommon bits then draw your line. Starting mask was /24, the new mask is /22.

So our new summarized address is 10.1.0.0/22

Once we drew our line, by looking from left to right on the third octet and stopping where the bits that go down the column are not common, we can clearly see that they are *0's* and *1's*. We now have our new subnet mask and as you can see, as all the bit values to the left of the line are all zeroes. This is precisely why we have "*zero*" in the third octet of the summary address. I hope you got it!

Nevertheless, let's see the actual range of this summary address using our subnetting method. What we are looking for is to see if we wasted any addresses or added another network in our summarization calculation. Did we?.. yes, no, maybe so?

First things first! As usual…draw your line and add your octets accordingly.

```
        4  3    255
10.1.000000 00.00000000
```

Network ID	Usable Range	Broadcast Address	CIDR
10.1.0.0	10.1.0.1 – 10.1.3.254	10.1.3.255	/22

Guys! See how beautifully it worked out? There was no wasting of IP addresses; you have exactly what you needed, and all the networks that you originally started with are within the range of the summary address (i.e.: under the /22 mask). So, you take that summary address of **10.1.0.0/22** and you would advertise it out through the interface connected to your core router to reduce the routing table. Below is an example of that command using EIGRP.

IP summary-address eigrp 100 10.1.0.0 255.255.252.0,

        Command   *Protocol AS*   *Summary-address*

But let's see a visual example of what we are talking about, using an actual topology.

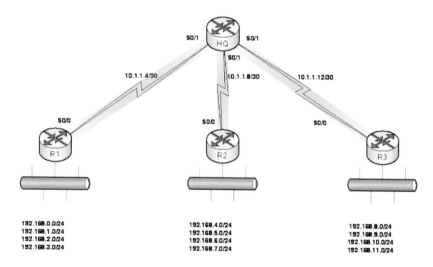

As you can see in the topology above, we only have two physical layers. The HQ router would represent the "Core Layer" and routers 1 – 3 would be considered "Distribution/Access Layer" routers. You can also see that all the LAN routers are connected directly into the core router, so if R1 wants to send a packet to R2 or R3 it would have to go through the HQ router, which means that the HQ router would have learned about all those networks through EIGRP, making the HQ router's routing table larger than it has to be.

This is how the routing table would look like before summarization in the HQ router:

HQ#SH IP ROUTE

Codes: C - connected, S - static, I - IGRP, R - RIP, M - mobile, B - BGP

D - EIGRP, EX - EIGRP external, O - OSPF, IA - OSPF inter area

N1 - OSPF NSSA external type 1, N2 - OSPF NSSA external type 2

E1 - OSPF external type 1, E2 - OSPF external type 2, E - EGP

i - IS-IS, L1 - IS-IS level-1, L2 - IS-IS level-2, ia - IS-IS inter area

* - candidate default, U - per-user static route, o - ODR

P - Periodic downloaded static route

Gateway of last resort is not set

10.0.0.0/30 is subnetted, 3 subnets

C   10.1.1.4 is directly connected, Serial0/0/0

C   10.1.1.8 is directly connected, Serial0/1/0

C   10.1.1.12 is directly connected, Serial0/2/0

D   192.168.0.0/24   [90/20514560]   via   10.1.1.5,   00:00:11, Serial0/0/0

D   192.168.1.0/24   [90/20514560]   via   10.1.1.5,   00:00:11, Serial0/0/0

*D   192.168.2.0/24   [90/20514560]   via   10.1.1.5,   00:00:11,
Serial0/0/0*

*D   192.168.3.0/24   [90/20514560]   via   10.1.1.5,   00:00:11,
Serial0/0/0*

*D   192.168.4.0/24   [90/20514560]   via   10.1.1.9,   00:00:11,
Serial0/1/0*

*D   192.168.5.0/24   [90/20514560]   via   10.1.1.9,   00:00:11,
Serial0/1/0*

*D   192.168.6.0/24   [90/20514560]   via   10.1.1.9,   00:00:11,
Serial0/1/0*

*D   192.168.7.0/24   [90/20514560]   via   10.1.1.9,   00:00:11,
Serial0/1/0*

*D   192.168.8.0/24   [90/20514560]   via   10.1.1.13,   00:00:11,
Serial0/2/0*

*D   192.168.9.0/24   [90/20514560]   via   10.1.1.13,   00:00:11,
Serial0/2/0*

*D   192.168.10.0/24   [90/20514560]   via   10.1.1.13,   00:00:11,
Serial0/2/0*

*D   192.168.11.0/24   [90/20514560]   via   10.1.1.13,   00:00:11,
Serial0/2/0*

For the purpose of the lab above, this is a lot of networks for the HQ routers to know about. The router would have to go through each one of these 15 entries to see where it needs to send the destination packet. However, we are going to help with that situation by summarizing each of the LAN's networks and advertising their summary address to the HQ router. This will reduce the amount of entries to the three learned routes and in turn, its three connected routes. Doing this will decrease the overhead and the router would only have to look at the three learned routes instead of twelve. So, how do we do this? Let's take a look, shall we?

Bear in mind that the starting mask is /24. Subsequently, we count left to right; you would start at the beginning of the third octet, which is the interesting octet.

The summary address 192.168.8.0/22

Now that we found our summary address by drawing the line between the common and un-common bits, its time to advertise to the HQ router through the interface that faces the HQ router. Following is the command you would use:

```
                                                          ┌──────────────────┐
                                                          │  Un-common bits  │
                                                          └──────────────────┘
LAN1(Bit Values are off)
192.168.0.0    x.x.000000|00.00000000
192.168.1.0    x.x.000000|01.00000000
192.168.2.0    x.x.000000|10.00000000
192.168.3.0    x.x.000000|11.00000000
Summary address 192.168.0.0/22

                                                          ┌──────────────────┐
                                                          │  Un-common bits  │
                                                          └──────────────────┘
LAN2  (Bit Value is on) 4
192.168.4.0    x.x.000001|00.00000000
192.168.5.0    x.x.000001|01.00000000
192.168.6.0    x.x.000001|10.00000000
192.168.7.0    x.x.000001|11.00000000
Summary address 192.168.4.0/22

                                                          ┌──────────────────┐
                                                          │  Un-common bits  │
                                                          └──────────────────┘
LAN3 (Bit Value is on) 8
192.168.8.0    x.x.000010|00.00000000
192.168.9.0    x.x.000010|01.00000000
192.168.10.0   x.x.000010|10.00000000
192.168.11.0   x.x.000010|11.00000000
```

LAN1

IP summary-address EIGRP 100 192.168.0.0 255.255.252.0

LAN2

IP summary-address EIGRP 100 192.168.4.0 255.255.252.0

LAN3

IP summary-address EIGRP: 100 192.168.8.0 255.255.252.0

Let's take a look at the HQ routers routing table after we advertise the summary routes.

HQ#sh ip route

Codes: C - connected, S - static, I - IGRP, R - RIP, M - mobile, B - BGP

D - EIGRP, EX - EIGRP external, O - OSPF, IA - OSPF inter area

N1 - OSPF NSSA external type 1, N2 - OSPF NSSA external type 2

E1 - OSPF external type 1, E2 - OSPF external type 2, E - EGP

i - IS-IS, L1 - IS-IS level-1, L2 - IS-IS level-2, ia - IS-IS inter area

* - candidate default, U - per-user static route, o - ODR

P - periodic downloaded static route

Gateway of last resort is not set

10.0.0.0/30 is subnetted, 3 subnets

C   10.1.1.4 is directly connected, Serial0/0/0

C   10.1.1.8 is directly connected, Serial0/1/0

C   10.1.1.12 is directly connected, Serial0/2/0

D   192.168.0.0/22   [90/20514560]   via   10.1.1.5,   00:02:08, Serial0/0/0

D   192.168.4.0/22   [90/20514560]   via   10.1.1.9,   00:01:05, Serial0/1/0

D   192.168.8.0/22   [90/20514560]   via   10.1.1.13,   00:00:15, Serial0/2/0

HQ#

Here you can see that we have three routes instead of twelve. For that reason, we are learning that through the routing protocol "EIGRP", your core router needs to only look at the 3 learned entries vs. 12! Isn't this so much better on your routers processor usage?

There you go! This is why and how we summarize...pretty simple right? I believe it's even easier than subnetting. *"really Laz?",* well, think about it? It's essentially the same process. All you have to do is find the *"magic"* line. In this case you draw the line between the common and uncommon bits and voila!...you're done. You have to admit. It doesn't get any easier than that.

Our next chapter is all about Wildcard Masking. I know what you're thinking *"Laz, are we taking a trip into the jungle?...get it? "wild = jungle" Oh well, I tried"* Anyway, we will take a JOURNEY into the world of Wildcard Masking, but it will be fun, easy but informative. You guys should know me by now.

However, before we do, let me show you one more example of summarization that you may find on your exam, but if you don't, consider yourself lucky, at least this will reiterate what I'm trying to convey.

| | Un-common bits |

192.168.1.4/30   X.X.X.00000100
192.168.1.8/30   X.X.X.00001000
192.168.1.12/30   X.X.X.00001100
192.168.1.16/30   X.X.X.00010000

As you can see, we started with a /30, but now we have a /27. This is how all these networks come together. All you have to do is follow the same concepts and you will be okay. Count from left to right until your reach the un-common bit values and draw your line, that's how you find your new mask. In return, the summary-address would be **192.168.1.0/27**. I hope that by now you have realized that this is really a piece of cake…not the complicated, theoretical equations with physics algorithms that other books, teachers and instructors have made it out to be. ;) Remember that my method is to teach you in a very simplistic manner so you can grasp and comprehend the concepts to be able to pass your CCNA certification exam, or your college exam, or whatever exam that would include questions on IP's. This is the sole purpose why I decided to write this book. I felt a need to demystify the whole intimidating scheme surrounding IP's.

IPv4 Wildcard Masking

What is it and where do we use them?

A Wildcard Mask is used in three different ways within the CCNA. One way is when configuring OSPF to identify which interfaces will take part in that particular OSPF process. The other way is when configuring NAT. This is when you are allowing a certain number of hosts to use the NAT router. The last but not least, is when creating a standard access-list and/or when using access-list to deny or permit access to certain destinations, port numbers and protocols.

A wildcard mask looks something like this; **0.0.0.255**. It's the opposite of a subnet mask. Except, what this particular "**Wildcard Mask**" is stating is the following; the zeros match the exact number that's in that specific octet, and 255 means that any range of numbers from 1-255 could fall in that particular octet. "*Hey Laz, that's fine and dandy, but how do we come up with a wildcard mask?*" Good question! There are two ways to come up with the wildcard mask. Here, I will show you both; all you need to do is choose the one that is easiest for YOU!

Remember when we were subnetting and we drew our line? Well, the sum of those bits to the right is how we came up with a value called the "*Broadcast Calculation Number*" right? ...guess what? ...that is also your "*wildcard mask*". Below I will show you some examples just to give you a visual on how it works:

Subnetmask	Binary	Wildcard Mask(sum of Bit values to the right of the line, PER OCTET)	CIDR
255.255.255.0	x.x.x.|00000000	0.0.0.255	/24
255.255.255.240	X.X.X.1111|0000	0.0.0.15	/28
255.255.255.252	X.X.X.111111|00	0.0.0.3	/30
255.255.224.0	X.X.111|00000.00000000	0.0.31.255	/19

How to use Wildcard Masking with OSPF

R1(config)#router ospf 1

R1(config-router)#network 10.1.1.4 0.0.0.3 area 51

How to use Wildcard Masking with ACL (Access-list)

First, to deny a particular host using a standard access-list you must do the following:

Access-list 1 deny 192.168.1.1 0.0.0.0

How to use Wildcard Masking with NAT

In NAT, you would do the same as above since you would be using a standard access list to permit a particular host(s) or network(s).

Access-list 1 permit 192.168.1.1 0.0.0.255

Oops...I did promise that I would show you two (2) ways of how to acquire a wildcard mask didn't I? Well, below, is the second method.

255.255.255.255 (This is a constant number that you subtract your mask from)

-255.255.255.224

0 . 0 . 0 . 31

There you go! Wildcard Masking, pretty straight forward isn't it?

Summary of IPv4

Since all good things must come to an end, this is no different. Here we have sort-of finalized our section on IPv4; we have covered IPv4 addresses, subnetting, VLSM, summarization and even Wildcard Masking. But it is going to be up to you to practice these skills on a daily basis or you will forget (*if you don't use it – you lose it!*).

Remember that a very miniscule amount of IPv6 addresses is currently being used worldwide. As a result, you still need to understand IPv4 until a complete transition has taken place, so please don't hold your breath, since this will not take place anywhere in the near future. IP is the fundamental protocol in any network. So you can either master IP addressing (*both, IPv4 & IPv6*) or prepare to be a slave to a subnet calculator (*If this is so, then, be prepared to be kicked out of the testing site when you decide to take the CCNA certification exam!*) It's as simple as that! All you're really doing is short changing yourself if you choose the latter. So, why go through the agony? Unless, of course, you're into that sort of thing. Hey, I don't judge! *To each his own.*

Now, don't misunderstand me either, although you will be tested on IPv4 to include subnetting an IPv4 address, you will not, however, (*for now anyway*) need to subnet an IPv6 address for the current CCNA test. Just know to identify it. But be prepared to have another test change in the future and I have a hunch that there will be more of IPv6 questions implemented when that change comes. That is why here, I am giving you a head start. ☺ If and when the time comes, you can just pull out this book from your bag of tricks, then you will have no problem passing the newer version as it pertains to IP's.

Remember, repetition breeds retention (*most of the time anyway – I've actually witnessed some exceptions to this rule*), however, this is something I learned in the military and I believe that it holds true for about 97.6% of the time. The more you do something, the more it's going to become second nature and the more you will retain the information. Unfortunately, IP seems to be the kryptonite to every IT individual out there...do not let it be yours. So practice!

If you also have the CD, the Audio File or the DVD for this book in which I am explaining each chapter here-in; please make sure that you listen closely to make sure that you understand the concepts taught in this section, because it does not stop here.

Going forward, we will now move into the *IPv6 part of this book*. So, tighten your seat belts, because here we go!

IPv6

The New Frontier

As I have stressed before, the mastering of IPv4 is essential before soaring into this vast and un-chartered "New Frontier" we call IPv6. So I hope you have already mastered IPv4 because we are now going to get very familiar with IPv6 and its components. Although, for the purpose of taking the CCNA certification exam all you really need is the basics. Don't freak out and think that you will be tested on the intricacies of IPv6 to include configuring and/or subnetting…it's not going to happen, not yet anyway!

So, let us continue and be somewhat exploratory shall we? IPv6 brings to us new features such as; auto-configuration, built in IPsec, smaller headers and obviously, the main reason that it came to its realization; which was the quantum leap into the numbers of IP addresses it generates within its 128 bit address. These new IPv6 addresses are numbers that they (*and I say that sparingly since I have no idea who **they** are…we shall refer to as the powers that be*), had to makeup words as, "Undecillion, Octillion, Zillion, etc." really? …how awe-inspiring! Our dictionaries are getting bigger by the day ever since we were introduced to the World Wide Web and the advancement of Technology.

Did you know that a new word is created every 98 minutes? The vast majority of these came to be when we entered the era of the Internet, Social Media and the warp speed of the expansion of Technology (*anyway, that's my theory and I'm going to stick to it*), just a little trivia. But once again, I digress. Let's go back to focusing on IPv6. Let us not forget that now, this new format of IP addressing is in hexadecimal format and it's a 128 bit address…this is huge isn't it? To put it into perspective, *and please don't quote me on this, since I heard it somewhere on the internet.*

Let's say that IPv4 was a grain of sand and it can fill a dump truck…in comparison, IPv6 is also a grain of sand but it can fill up the sun! Whom ever came up with IPv6 must have thought that the issue of running out of IP addresses was going to be fixed once and for all for generations to come. So, this ginormous amount of IPv6 addresses are not going to be exhausted any time soon. At least not in mine, yours, your child's or your child's child life time!

But, do we really need a billion, billion addresses for every individual on the planet? Well, if the intent was indeed to deter us from mastering IPv6, it did NOT WORK ON ME! I actually welcome this challenge with open arms. This is awesome!…and this book will help you dominate and conquer this new and exciting new Internet Protocol just as you did with IPv4.

You will learn, not only the new types of addresses, how their formatted, the different ways of assigning these addresses, configuring the new routing protocols that had to be updated for IPv6, but best of all, how to subnet this enormous address. *Scared yet?* I can sense some of you are just scratching your heads aren't you? *Hey…don't fear Laz is here!* I know what you are thinking *"subnetting in hex? …you must be crazy!"* I say to you now, that by the time you finish the journey into IPv6 as explained in this book, you will come out the other side triumphant! Not only will you fully understand IPv6, how to subnet in IPv6 and so on, but you will also know how to apply its concepts in the real world. So enough words on the subject and let's start marching forward towards glory!

Do We Really Need IPv6?

Unquestionably! We desperately need IPv6. Just the fact that Cisco announced, in one of their webinars in 2013, that it was going to be the last year for public IPv4 addresses, is more than enough reason to transition to IPv6. We literary have run out of public IPv4 address and we have an obligation to keep up with the change in new and emerging technologies. With IPv4 (*you know, the one with the 32 bit address*), it only allots for a meager 4.2 billion addresses in total worldwide. That was fine and dandy at one point, but the world population has continued to grow and has now surpassed an astounding 7 billion, without any ending in sight. Definitely not enough addresses in IPv4 to appease the ever growing population of internet and technology users, (*no one saw this coming!*). For this very reason, NAT and VLSM were created. These protocols were meant to slow down the inevitable demise of the public IPv4 addresses. However, as they say "*all good things must come to an end*" thus, here we are.

So, who will come to save us from this trepidation? ...*ta-ta-ra-da*...IPv6 to the RESCUE!!! With its 128 bits, holding an astounding *340 Undecillion* total addresses, or to be exact; **340,282,366,920,938,463,463,374,607,431,768,211,456** quiet the pay check right? You now have the possibility for each person in the world to have, as many as 15 quintillion addresses or to be exact once more; **18,446,744,073,709,552,000** on just one network. I think we are pretty much covered on IP's for a long time to come don't you?

Once we start colonizing other worlds, then we may need IPv7 or even 8 or... maybe not! Think about it? We, as individuals and for personal uses have at least two devices that we own that need an IP address. Our tablets, our PC's, our cell phones (whether *it's a smart phone or not*), our home phones (*do we still have those?...believe it or not, my mother has one, with the same phone number since the 1970's!*), etc. Not to mention businesses that have multiple PC's, printers, faxes, plotters, switches, routers, etc... so, do we need IPv6 in our networks? MOST DEFINITELY! "*Laz, tell us the benefits of IPv6*". I'm glad you asked.

What are the benefits of using IPv6?

One thing we can always guarantee in life is that "CHANGE" will always happen. It's just inevitable…(i.e.: our bodies change as we get older, our relationships change as time goes by, our jobs and titles change as companies implement new technologies, the CCNA certification exam changed from the (640-802) to the new one you will take now, the (200-120)…see, everything changes) However, some of us resist change. That is what I like to call **TCRS** or "*The Change Resistance Syndrome*"…here you go Wikipedia – add that to your list!

I saw this happen when we were going from NT4 to NT5 which was WIN2K, (*if you are a millennial, then most likely you do not know what that is; this is meant for the dinosaurs in the room*). Wow! We dreaded that change didn't we? We thought that nothing could improve NT4 right?...*WRONG!* I remember the complaints and the resistance to change then as I still see the resistance now; not just from employees either, but also from employers. TCRS was entrenched back then as it is today. I know it's difficult, but hey, you must adapt and overcome this fear of change. After all, you can't stop it, so you might as well embrace it, or at least try. If you listen to the naysayers, you know, those that will try to convince you that there are NO new benefits to IPv6 then you will be lost, confused, aggravated and stressed out. Why put yourself through the ringer about something that is inevitable and ultimately simple to learn. So, to those individuals out there, and believe me, you will encounter plenty; I want you to respond in an informed and competent manner (…don't worry, this book will get you there), and let them know that YES, there are plenty of benefits to switching to IPv6. I want you to then proceed to point out the benefits that IPv6 brings; for example: we have IPsec built in that provides end to end security, a header that is half the size of IPv4, and since its aligned to 64 bits, it will increase the processing speed significantly as well. Of course we know the awe-inspiring number of IP's that would now allow for more efficient routing, and lets not forget the new types of addresses such as *"Anycast"* known also as *"One to Nearest"*, and hallelujah…no more BROADCAST! It is all now *"Multicast"* and you could have many different types of addresses on the same interface; **Unicast**, **Multicast**, and **Anycast**. I know what you're thinking. *"Man, this is awesome!"* YES IT IS!

I would of course like to mention the *Link-local* address, but, that will always be present on your PC regardless of DHCP or not; this will be present on your router's interface as well. Just wanted to throw that out there just as an FYI. ☺

So, mark my words, IPv6 is chalk full of benefits and enhancements that will be most advantageous to us all.

The assignment of these addresses are different as well, let me explain; we could assign the IP address statically, both the Network Prefix and Interface ID, followed by its prefix-length, or we could just put the network prefix portion of the address followed by a double colon and ending it with the prefix-length, whatever it may be.

In order to generate the Interface ID portion of it, we would use another new feature called auto-configuration which is typing this command: *eui-64* after the prefix length. It will generate the Interface ID portion of the address using the MAC address of the routers interface. That will only give us a 48 bit address. But hey!...we need 64 bits. So, to accommodate for the missing bits, it will **pad** the MAC address with the following: *FFFE* to the middle of the address, meaning it will insert the *FFFE* smack in the middle of the MAC address to make it 64 bits.

So, most definitely IPv6 brings its benefits; this is but a nibble of all the benefits it brings. But it's enough for what we need to know for certification purposes and employment needs for now.

Now, let's start looking at these addresses and how they are made-up.

Addressing and Expressions

Remember IPv6 addresses are in hexadecimal format, and they are separated into 8 sections of 4 hexadecimal numbers separated by colons. This creates our 128 bit address.

Example:

2001:3200:0abc:1100:0000:0000:1234:abc1/64

Do not let the size of this address deter you from your goal! We will dissect this type of address and understand what we are looking at, to include the make-up of this 128 bit address.

An IPv6 address is really broken into two parts, the first part is made up of four (4) sections. This part is called the **Network Prefix**. The next part also has four (4) sections and is called the **Interface ID.** The 2nd part of the address (*Interface ID*), can be generated automatically using the *eui-64* command. The **/64** is also called the prefix-length, this is NOT a subnet mask as it was in IPv4.

FYI: *The word CIDR is use in IPv4 only and is therefore considered an archaic terminology. This is used for routing purposes only and it has nothing to do with the Interface ID of the address.*

Let us breakdown the above address into its two parts and then further breakdown each section of the Network Prefix portion of the address as follows:

2001	3200	0abc	1100	0000	0000	1234	abc1
Network Prefix 64 Bits				Interface ID 64 Bits			

Once again remember that the values you are looking at are *hexadecimal* values! Each one of those numbers or letters really represents 4 bits...you didn't forget, did you? You need to understand that, this is how each section equates to **16 bits**.

Now let's take the Network Prefix and place each section into its category:

2001	3200	0abc	1100
Registry	ISP	Company	Subnet

In IPv6 we do not have "Classes" of addresses. What we do have in IPv6 is designation of addresses.

Let's consider the figure above...this is an example of a **Global Unicast** address. How do we know this? Well, this is simple. You should immediately recognize this by just looking at the first section of the address. Global Unicast addresses starts with **2001.** This means that you need to be able to look at an IPv6 address and be able to snap your fingers and know what type of address it is without dwelling too much on it. Take my word for it, this will become second nature to you as you practice and read this book a few times.

If the address would have started with **FE80**, then you would have known that the IPv6 address would be considered a **Link-**

local address instead. So in order to identify an IPv6 address we would look at the first section of the network prefix.

We will take a look at the different types of addresses further in this book.

Isn't this address just too big to type every time you need it? It certainly is! We need to make things fast and simple in order to be able to spend our precious time doing other things rather than typing these 128 bit addresses over and over again. *"Is there a shorter method to these addresses?* Thank goodness there is! "*The powers that be*" must have read our minds and actually thought the same thing. They came up with a fantastic way to shorten the expression and alleviate our fingers in the process. However, like everything in IT, it has rules that must be followed:

Rules

1. There can only be one (1) set of double colons- *NO EXCEPTIONS*

2. You can only remove leading zeroes from the address.

3. The complete address must equate to eight sections.

4. You can only go up to *F* in the hex table. *"This one is just common sense".*

Using the same address let's see how we can shorten it.

2001:3200:0abc:1100:0000:0000:1234:abc1/64

(Numbers highlighted in red can be removed.)

2001:3200:abc:1100::1234:abc1/64

We have removed all leading zeroes and the two sets of contiguous zeroes by using one double colon, this is a valid IPv6 address.

So what would an invalid IPv6 address look like?

Here is an example:
2001::HE35::1569:BEEF

The address above is breaking all the rules isn't it? First we have 2 sets of double colons, you should know that only one (1) set of double colons is permitted. So, why is that wrong? First of all, the protocol would not know where to place the zeroes, and secondly, hex numbers don not go beyond the letter "F". In this example, we see the letter "H" in the address, and it looks like we only have 6 sections instead of eight, but that could be due to the double colons that represent consecutive zeroes right? None the less, the above address is invalid one way or another and cannot be used.

Recognizing a valid & invalid address is extremely important when taking your certification exam. I do not want you to get points taken off for something as simple as this.

FYI: *You can have upper case and lower case hex in the address (as the examples above indicate), it does NOT make a difference as far as configuration is concerned...it is a matter of preference. Having said that, Cisco recommends that you keep the hex letters in lower case. In this book I do both. The upper case is mainly to make a visual emphasis. But, again, please follow the rules and do what Cisco recommends, why be defiant? After all, you need to get your CCNA.*

If asked, how can we fix this invalid address? Well, let's give it a try shall we?

2001:0:CE35:0:1569:BEEF::1

Here, I added a zero were the double colons were. From there on I had no idea about the rest of the address. Therefore, I simply put a double colon to represent a section of zeroes, and ended the address with a 1, which in turn would give us the Interface ID portion of the address to complete the eight sections needed. I also took the "H" and replaced it with a "C"...which is now a true value in the hex table to make this address valid.

Again, I did this to show the difference between a valid IPv6 address and an invalid IPv6 address to drive the message that, you need to recognize the difference between the two.

Expect to be asked the difference between valid & an invalid IPv6 address in the Cisco certification exam.

Types of Addresses in IPv6

All right, let's take a look at some of the addresses you need to be familiar with and their intended purposes.

The table below will help you with this:

Link-Local FE80::/10	This is the new **APIPA** and it is not routable. But it is always present on an interface. It uses Zone ID's, if multiple NICs exist on the device, to send the packet out through the correct interface.
Unique Local FC00::/7	This is a **Unique Local Address**. It is comparable to the private IPv4 addresses. It replaced the FC00::/10 Site local address in Sept 2004, there

	is also an FD00::/8 for a /48 prefix and FC00::/8 still in the works.
Multicast FF00::/8	This address is the same as in IPv4 *multicast address*. You will see these addresses quite often between all routing protocols when they send their updates. RIP: *FF02::/9* EIGRP: *FF02::A* OSPF: *FF02::5*
Anycast address	This address is also called the "*one to nearest*", which means; when a data packet is sent, based on the routing protocol, it will find the closest destination specified address and send the packet. These addresses come out of the range of the unique local range. Here is an example on how one would create it: *IPv6 address - 2002:0db8:6301::/128 anycast* The *anycast* command is the key, in order to make it work.
Special Addresses	
0:0:0:0:0:0:0:0	This could also be denoted as :: It equals the IPv4 address 0.0.0.0
0:0:0:0:0:0:0:1	This is the **Loopback** address in IPv6 and it is the only Loopback address. This is unlike IPv4 which took the entire 127 range. You could also

	express it as- **::1**. Done by removing the leading zeros.
0:0:0:0:0:0:0:0:10.1.1.1	Mixed environment using IPv6 with IPv4
2000::/3	Global unicast address range
3FFF:FFF:/32	Reserved for examples and Documentation
2001:0D88::/32	Same as above
2002::/16	This range is used for the transition mechanism- 6 to 4 tunneling.

To reiterate and as a finishing note on these addresses; all you would need to know is how to identify them. Are they a **Link-Local Address**, **Multicast**, **Global Unicast**, or **Loopback**? Remember that you will also be asked to identify a valid address; i.e.: no double colons, values above **F** and so forth. Please try to remember these basic addresses for the test.

I know that it's a totally different story once you get to the workplace, since that's where the real fun begins, but do not concern with that now since you need to pass a certification first.

Statically Assigning addresses

Assigning IPv6 addresses to a router is pretty much the same thing as in IPv4; but instead of typing *IP address:*

192.168.1.1 255.255.255.0

You would type *IPv6 address:*
2001:3200:0abc:1100:0000:0000:1234:abc1/64.

However, try using the shortened expression wherever possible, meaning, get rid of the leading zeroes and all consecutive zeroes were possible. Learning this will make your life a whole lot easier…and remember that you will learn it with practice.

When using IPv6, there is no need to type "*IPv6 enable*" on the interface unless you want to specifically use the *Link-local* address only. Once you type-in the complete address manually, it will enable IPv6.

CAUTION! Doing this command will not enable routing of the IPv6 addresses. Confused? Don't worry, we will talk about that later on.

Using the EUI-64

Another way you could assign IPv6 addresses is by using the *eui-64* command. This works by generating the *Interface ID* portion of the address automatically. It uses the MAC address of the interface to perform this task. "*But wait Laz, that's only 48 bits - we need 64*" There's a simple explanation to this as well. Let me explain; what **eui-64** does in order to make it a 64 bit address is to **PAD** or insert an **FFFE** in-between the MAC address.

The main concern here should be with your MAC address being part of the IPv6 complete address. But if your security is in place, (*...and it better be if you care about your job*), then you should have nothing to worry about. You should only be concerned with two things; "what does the command do? And how to configure it.

The following is an example of using the eui-64 command:

```
Router(config)#int g0/0
Router(config-if)#ipv6 address 2001:3200:1234:2100::/52 eui-64
Router(config-if)#
```

The following output would be the result of using the **eui-64** command.

```
Router#sh ipv6 int brief
GigabitEthernet0/0      [up/up]
    FE80::260:70FF:FEAE:B501 (link-local always present)
    2001:3200:1234:2000:260:70FF:FEAE:B501 (create the Interface ID)
```

DHCPv6

Well DHCP is pretty much DHCP; whether it's IPv4 or IPv6. It still does what it knows how to do best - *lease addresses*. Obviously we need to understand that we are now doing it for IPv6. Nonetheless, there are still a few limitations within the IOS of a Cisco router for DHCPv6; including DHCPv6 stateless support.

Know this, DHCP servers will be around for a bit. They are not going to disappear just yet so you must make sure you are still up to date when it comes to setting one up.

In my very humble opinion, I would shy away from setting up a router with the DHCP service enabled. My reasoning behind this is simply due to broadcasting to lease an address and also because of the continuous renewal of that address. I believe routers have more important tasks to perform than assigning IP addresses. *But hey...that's me!*

You can always set it up as a Relay Agent, using the ***IP-helper*** command on an interface, so it can go on behalf of the client to an actual DHCP server and have an IP address assigned to the client.

Yet again…no one should be going across broadcast domains to have IP address assigned to them; most specifically if it's across a WAN. The only way I can justify turning a router into a DHCP server is, if it's a small company. And even then, I have my reservations on that.

IPv6 Makeup

IPv6 Header vs. IPv4 Header

Version	Class	Flow Label	
Payload Length		Next Header	Hop Limit
Source Address 16 bytes, 128 bits			
Destination Address 16 bytes, 128 bits			

Version	Header Length	Priority and TOS	Total Length
Identification	Flags	Fragmented Offset	
TTL	Protocol	Header Checksum	
Source IP address			
Destination IP address			
Options			
Data			

Not to go into too much detail, just looking at the different headers, you can see that IPv4 is twice as big, but yet it's only 32 bits long. Where, the IPv6 header is half the size, and its 128 bits.

What does that tell you? Well, that IPv6 is more streamlined and that all the unwanted fields where taken out. Nonetheless, you do have optional extension headers after these eight (8) fields which carry Layer 3 information and they are not fixed.

That's really the basic difference between the two protocols. Please, do not go insane trying to memorize each field.

ICMPv6

ICMPv6 does pretty much the same tasks that its predecessor did with some extra features built-in.

TRIVIA: *You will NOT be asked this in a certification! You can just use it to impress your friends or co-workers.*

Did you know that the ICMPv6 packet is identified by the value **58** in the **next header** field of the ICMP message being sent?

The following you DO need to know:

When an ICMPv6 is traversing the network, it bases its MTU from its home link. If it encounters an MTU smaller than its own, one of the routers will send back a message "**packet too big**" to the originating machine. That will continue until the packets meet the MTU size criteria. At that time, all other data will pass without any fragmentation occurring.

ICMP is now being used for various task such as the following:

- Router Solicitation (RS)
- Router Advertisement (RA)
- Neighbor Solicitation (NA)
- Neighbor Advertisement (NA)
- Duplicate Address Detection (DAD)

One huge task is finding the neighbors' address on the same segment. Remember, there is no more broadcast – It is now all **multicast**. Therefore, when communicating between PC's we now have the NS and NA. If, on the other hand, communication is going to occur between a PC and a router, then we have RS and RA.

We also have DAD or *Duplicate Address Detecti*on. Really? With the amount of IP's we have available with IPv6 it is highly doubtful that we will have duplicate addresses on the network. But hey... stranger things have happened. And just in case this anomaly occurs, they came up with DAD. Just so you know, this is not a separate protocol. It is a function of the NS and NA messages.

As usual, DAD goes out along with the Neighbor Discovery Protocol/Neighbor Solicitation message asking if anyone has the same address.

IPv6 Routing Protocols and Configurations

As you might have noticed by now, I just can't get away from talking about routing! I love this subject and this is what Cisco is all about isn't it? ☺

In IPv6 we still have our static and dynamic routing, and as I like to call it, it's also the facelift of the IPv4 protocol. Both protocols essentially do the same thing, nonetheless, they are configured a bit differently.

This routing protocol…and *I'm talking about IPv6*, is configured on an interface-by-interface basis instead of a network statement *(or command),* as in IPv4.

So, let's go ahead and get started with static routing first.

Static Routing

The topology below is what we will be working with. This is where we need to make PC1 ping PC2 using static routes.

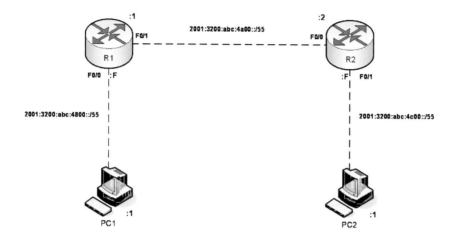

The first step would be to configure our PC's with their IPv6 addresses, prefix numbers and default gateways.

Following would be the configurations for each one of the PC's.

PC1

IPv6 address: 2001:3200:abc:4800::1/55

Default Gateway: 2001:3200:abc:4800::F/55

PC2

IPv6 address: 2001:3200:abc:4c00::1/55

Default Gateway: 2001:3200:abc:4c00::F/55

The second step would be to configure the routers interfaces to first have connectivity with each other.

The following would be an example on how to assign the IPv6 addresses statically to the routers interfaces with their appropriate prefix-length and consequently turning on their interface.

>enable

#config t

(config)#hostname R1

R1(config)#int f0/0

R1(config-if)#ipv6 address 2001:3200:abc:4800::F/55

R1(config-if)#no shut

R1(config-if)#int f0/1

R1(config-if)#ipv6 address 2001:3200:abc:4a00::1/55

R1(config-if)#no shut

R1(config-if)#do wr

>enable

#config t

(config)#hostname R2

R2(config)#int f0/0

R2(config-if)#ipv6 address 2001:3200:abc:4a00::2/55

R2(config-if)#no shut

R2(config-if)#int f0/1

R2(config-if)#ipv6 address 2001:3200:abc:4c00::F/55

R2(config-if)#no shut

R2(config-if)#do wr

Now that you have the routers configured, you need to make sure you can ping from router to router and that your PC's can reach their gateways. This will rule out any miss-configurations.

Once you have verified that indeed you can ping, it is time to start configuring the static route – *there's only two (2) here, so let's thank the heavens for that!*

You should already know that you need to turn on IPv6 **unicast-routing** *(it is turned off by default- this is essential for routing to occur in IPv6)*...now, let's get started.

R1(config)#ipv6 unicast-routing

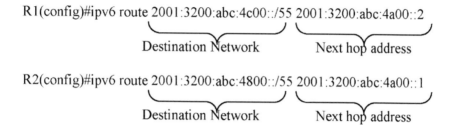

Here, all you need to do is **ping** and *VOILA!* You have connectivity within your enterprise!

Can you see the picture here? Static routing creates less overhead on your router. On the other hand, that does not hold true for the administrator. Especially if you are doing IPv6. It was quite easy to do static routing in our example since it had only one static route. But just imagine 10, 30 or in certain companies 100's if not 1,000's of static routes. If that's the case, then copy & paste will become your next best friend.

But let's continue. Too many static routes can lend to user error. You can very easily forget to enter a static route or configure it incorrectly. I myself have experienced this personally. *It's just part of being human...but try to minimize that trait.*

When you get to that time in your life to do routing protocols such as; RIPng, EIGRPv6 and OSPFv3 instead of static routing, you could have a combination of any of these on your routers.

However, on the stub routers (*these are the edge routers that have only one way in and one way out of the network*), you would use *"**Default Static Routes***" also…but that's another book I'll be writing.

Dynamic Routing

In dynamic routing the protocols algorithm still remains the same; meaning, the way it calculates the best path to a destination does not change. What does change however, is how you configure it.

We will use the same topology as before, the only difference is that you will configure RIPng.

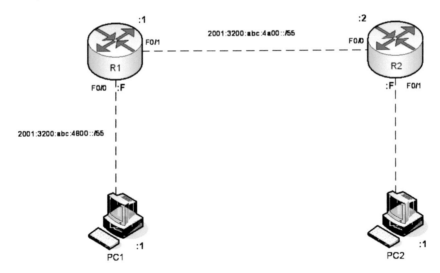

The first thing we have to get rid of, are the static routes. Keep in mind that static routes have a lower administrative distance

(AD) than any routing protocol. *(If you do not get rid of the static routes, they will always get preference to populate the routing table).* Unless you want to keep them as a back-up. At that point you would have to increase the AD to a number higher than the routing protocol you are using; in this case higher than RIP. This is then added at the end of the *"IPv6 Static Route Statement"*.

Below is an example:

R1(config)#ipv6 route 2001:3200:abc:4c00::/55 2001:3200:abc:4a00::2 *150*.

If you do not take out the static routes, RIPng will never make it to the routing table.

The following is the command you would type to remove the static routes' entries:

R1(config)#no ipv6 route 2001:3200:abc:4c00::/55 2001:3200:abc:4a00::2

R2(config)#no ipv6 route 2001:3200:abc:4800::/55 2001:3200:abc:4a00::1

Looking at the commands above, you can see that by just adding the word "**no**" in front of your static route, it removes it. Just in case you were wondering…yes, you must type the whole statement for it to work. Always cross-check your work to make sure that it indeed worked by typing *show run* or *show start*. Remember to *"trust but verify!"*

Now, let's configure RIPng on both routers. This time though, instead of advertising the networks that you are attached to, you actually go into the interfaces that you want to participate in the RIP process and enable it. You still have enable RIPng Globally but the network entries are gone and so is the command no auto-summary.

Let us see how this is done:

R1(config)#ipv6 router rip 1 ⟶ This number identifies a process for RIP
R1(config-router)#int f0/0
R1(config-if)#ipv6 router rip 1 enable
R1(config-if)#int f0/1
R1(config-if)#ipv6 router rip 1 enable ⟶ The number in the interface must match the
Process number you entered in global config

R2(config)#ipv6 router rip 1
R2(config-router)#int f0/0
R2(config-if)#ipv6 router rip 1 enable
R2(config-if)#int f0/1
R2(config-if)#ipv6 router rip 1 enable

That's all there is to it...you're done! I know it looks funny, especially the number one (1). All that really does is identifies the process for the particular instance of RIP (*this can be different for every router*), however, it is locally significant. Just make sure that whatever number you enable RIP with is in global configuration; you have to use the same number on the interfaces (*these number must ALWAYS match*).

Next we have OSPF; the topology still remains the same. But this time we do not need to remove RIP; because the AD of RIP is 120, and the AD of OSPF is 110. Since OSPF has a lower AD, it will have preference over RIP to populate the routing table. Once again, you could change the AD of any routing protocol by going into router configuration mode of that specific routing protocol.

So let's see how you would configure OSPF:

```
R1(config)#ipv6 router ospf 1
R1(config-router)#router-id 1.1.1.1
R1(config-router)#int f0/0
R1(config-if)#ipv6 ospf 1 area 51     The area number must be the same on all
routers
R1(config-if)#int f0/1
R1(config-if)#ipv6 ospf 1 area 51

R2(config)#ipv6 router ospf 1
R2(config-router)#router-id 2.2.2.2     The RID can be different per router.
R2(config-router)#int f0/0
R2(config-if)#ipv6 ospf 1 area 51
R2(config-if)#int f0/1
R2(config-if)#ipv6 ospf 1 area 51
```

See how simple it is…you are now done! I always like to use addresses like the ones you see in the example as my Router ID. Usually, this would be my Loopback address on the router. The loopback address normally matches according to the number of the router as well. Please don't forget that all routers must be in the same area; that is a key factor in the CCNA. Also, always verify by pinging and using the command *show ipv6 route* to look at your routing table.

Okay, we made it to the last routing protocol required for the CCNA…EIGRPv6! And once again, we do not need to remove any of the routing protocols we configured because EIGRP's AD is 90, which is lower than RIP and OSPF. That means it will take over the routing table. With this routing protocol, we need to use an autonomous system which has to be the same across all routers. Nonetheless, we have to give it a Router-ID which defines a **"Protocol Instance"**. We would also need to turn the protocol **"on"** by doing the *no shut* command within the router configuration mode. Once that's done, we can go to the interfaces and enable it on the ones we want to participate in the EIGRP process.

93

```
R1(config)#ipv6 router eigrp 100
R1(config-router)#router-id 1.1.1.1    RID signifies a protocol instance
R1(config-router)#no shut
R1(config-router)#int f0/0
R1(config-router)#ipv6 eigrp 100
R1(config-router)#int f0/1
R1(config-router)#ipv6 eigrp 100    AS number must be the same on all routers

R2(config)#ipv6 router eigrp 100
R2(config-router)#router-id 2.2.2.2
R2(config-router)#no shut
R2(config-router)#int f0/0
R2(config-router)#ipv6 eigrp 100
R2(config-router)#int f0/1
R2(config-router)#ipv6 eigrp 100
```

Do not wait for the routing protocol to converge. Run your command *show ipv6 route* and you should see your D's in the routing table.

IPv6 routing is really not that much different than in IPv4. The concepts stay the same and to be honest it makes more sense now.

Now that we are familiar with IPv6, we come to the biggest topic yet, of course I'm talking about **subnetting**. I hope you are ready and excited as I am, because our journey continues.

IPv6 Subnetting

In the world of IPv4 subnetting, (*as you saw here, it was not as difficult as you thought right?*), we had to pay attention to a lot of things that we do not need to concern ourselves with now with IPv6. One of these being the number of hosts we needed. In IPv4 subnetting, we had to make sure that we used the correct subnet mask to segment our network properly and provide enough host for that segment for future growth. Therefore, subnetting in IPv4 sometimes made the network somewhat complex and even more difficult to manage. At least that has been my personal experience.

Now with IPv6 we do not have those concerns, do we? We only pay attention to the Network Prefix of the address, this is the first 64 bits of the address. The /64 is NOT a subnet mask anymore. In IPv6 it's now called a Prefix-length and it deals with the routing process. No longer do we have to worry if we have enough host addresses. *This is awesome!* If you remember earlier in this book, I stated that one IPv6 address has 15 quintillion addresses. I think that speaks for itself don't you think? What I'm trying to convey here is that we no longer have to worry about the Interface ID side of the address.

What throws most people aback with IPv6 addresses and subnetting is the 128 bit address and that it is in hexadecimal format. I know it looks insane, but, *"do not fear – Laz is here!"* And just like in IPv4 you will use the same method to subnet in IPv6.

You also need to remember that the 4th section of the Network Prefix of an IPv6 address is what has been allotted for you to subnet. This will be the section you will be working with.

Example 1:   **2001:3200:1600:2000::/51**

This is the address you have been given and you must subnet it, into 8 subnets.

How do we attack this problem?

Take the 4th section, which is highlighted in red, and separated into binary format.

2	0	0	0
0010	0000	0000	0000
1st Position	2nd Position	3rd Position	4th Position

Above is how the **2000** would look in its binary format; remember each one of those numbers is comprised of 4 bits that represent a section of 16 bits, which in turn gives us 65,536 networks to work with. By the third section, you have a prefix length of **/48**.

But wait! You were given a prefix length of **/51** as a starting point right? This means, you cannot use anything smaller than **/51**. This is the starting point for you to subnet in IPv6. Here is where our handy dandy "**magic line**" comes into play; once you have that taken care of, you then start counting from 49 until you reach 51. Once this is done, you can then begin counting for your eight subnets as shown below:

```
   Start point
  8 4 2 = bit values
  000|0   00|00   0000   0000   (Note: this is the 4th Section)
      2      4 8 = subnets
```

What you are trying to find is the increment number. In this scenario, it is the bit highlighted in red, which has a value of 4 in the 2nd Position. Therefore, we had to turn on 3 more bits to be able to have 8 subnets which in turn gave us the new Prefix-length of **/54**.

Let us take a look at how our new subnets would look like:

2001:3200:1600:2000::/51 (**Note:** *this is the starting point*)

2001:3200:1600:2000::/54
2001:3200:1600:2400::/54
2001:3200:1600:2800::/54
2001:3200:1600:2C00::/54
2001:3200:1600:3000::/54
2001:3200:1600:3400::/54
2001:3200:1600:3800::/54
2001:3200:1600:3C00::/54

See…it is the same exact concept as in IPv4. You count for your subnets from left to right and draw your line. The bit value to the left of the line is your network increment, the only difference now is that we increment in Hex.

As you can see in this problem our increment is 4 in the 2nd Position. For that reason, just keep adding 4 to the second number from left to right and that is how you get your values.

The tricky part is that now, you are dealing with letters. Let's not forget your hex table as previously mentioned, but just in case you did, I have included it here again:

Hex Table

0	0
1	1
2	2
3	3
4	4
5	5
6	6
7	7
8	8
9	9
A	10
B	11
C	12
D	13
E	14
F	15

So if you take the following number:
2000 and you increment by 4 in the 2nd position it equals.
+400
2400

Let's try another example:
2800
+400
2C00?   8+4=12 which is C then simply lower the 2

One more example:
2C00
+400
3000?   C+4=16 this goes over the max value of 15
So you would reset the 2nd Position column
To zero and add 1 to the first position column.

Let's take a look at another example, just to drill it in:

In the following example, your starting address will be the following:

2001:4800:2201:1000::/48.

In this example you were given a prefix-length of **/48** and a starting value of **1000**. We would like to subnet this address into 6 subnets.

I am using small numbers throughout this book just so you can become familiar with the concepts of subnetting in IPv6. Ultimately, practicing over and over will make you a master at it, at that point you will be able to subnet with more complex addresses. By that time you will be doing subnetting in your sleep.

```
8421    8421    8421    8421
|000|0  0000    0000    0000
 246
```

(The first line is the /48 starting point)

Let's practice one more time!

Once again…below, we are looking for the increment number. *Which is the bit value to the left of the line.* In this case, that number is 2 in the 1st Position.

2001:4800:2201:1000::/48 (*This is the starting address*)

2001:4800:2201:1000::/51
2001:4800:2201:3000::/51
2001:4800:2201:5000::/51
2001:4800:2201:7000::/51
2001:4800:2201:9000::/51
2001:4800:2201:b000::/51

Well, there you have it! You needed 6 subnets; so you turned on 3 more bits which now gave you a prefix length of 51. As you can see in the 4th Section you are incrementing by two in the 1st Position.

This is just the tip of the iceberg ladies & gentlemen, there is a lot more to it than this. However, this is the basic fundamentals that you need to know, not only for the CCNA certification exam, but also for hiring purposes. Notice that you can now do it without having to use those weird classical mechanics computations.

"Laz, will I be asked to subnet in IPv6 for the CCNA exam?" For now, I highly doubt it. But if they do…this book will be your guide to take any IP test with confidence. It is the only IP book you will ever need!

Hex conversions for fun

Let's finish off the book with some easy and fun conversions; especially now that we are using IPv6. Wouldn't it would be fun to learn how to convert hex numbers just for the hell of it? I want you to be an expert in IP's; but would also like you to be familiar with conversions as well. *I'm here to tell you that you can count on me for support.* ☺

Okay now…remember that we have different bases of numbers we use; base **16** which is **hex**, base **10** which is **decimal**, and base **2** which is **binary**. I will show you how you can easily go back and forth from one to the other without complicated formulas.

Below again, are a couple of things you need to know or should already know:

Hex Table

0	0
1	1
2	2
3	3
4	4
5	5
6	6
7	7
8	8
9	9
A	10
B	11
C	12
D	13
E	14
F	15

Bit Values

128	64	32	16	8	4	2	1

Let's convert the following decimal number to Hex: **152**
Binary is always the middle ground, so using the bit value table above is how we will turn 152 into binary.

128	64	32	16	8	4	2	1

Turning on those bit values equates to 152… in binary it looks like this:

10010100

Turning it to hex, we break the eight bits into two parts of four bits:

1001 | 0100
8 4 2 1   8 4 2 1

You would add the bit values that are "**on**" for each section:

1001 | 0100
8 4 2 1   8 4 2 1
    9   4

The Hex number would be **94**! You would write it in the following format: **0x94**.

The "**0x**" is an *identifier* to let you know that what you're looking at is a HEX number.

Pretty easy right? It just doesn't get any easier than this!

Let's do a different example.

This time, let's convert a hex number to a decimal: **E5**

E   5
1110   0101
8 4 2 1   8 4 2 1

Now you would add the bit values that are "**on**" and bring them together as one:

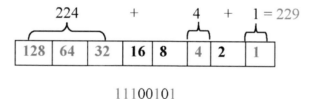

11100101

If you add all the bit values that are *on*…you get a grand total of **229**.

That's all there is to it! Just remember to convert first to binary, then to hex or decimal.

You must commit the Hex table, bit values and bit to decimal table to memory. There is no getting around it, if you want to make your life easy - JUST DO IT!

Just in case you don't remember reading earlier about the bit to decimal, here it is again:

Binary	Bit	Decimal
10000000	1	128
11000000	2	192
11100000	3	224
11110000	4	240
11111000	5	248
11111100	6	252
11111110	7	254
11111111	8	255

Summary of IP's

There you have it, IPv4 & IPv6 in a nut shell! We've gone through the addressing part of both protocols and their features. I've also shown you how to configure with step-by-step instructions for all three routing protocols: RIPng, OSPv3 and EIGRPv6. But the best part of all is that we made it through the subnetting portion of it fairly easy-for both IPv4 & IPv6. We then finished off with a little fun with Hex conversions as well.

Please remember that even though we were having fun with converting hex, decimals and binary numbers, it is crucial that you become very familiar with this more than ever before since the IP's of the future will be all in HEX!

Making the move to the IPv6 protocol will definitely make our networks more robust in their routing and will bring a new era of subnetting.

The Start of a New Beginning!

Although IPv4 may be phasing out as IPv6 is being implemented, we should note that it's an opportunity for all of us in the IT field to feel good that there will now be enough IP's for everyone in the globe to be connected! The end of an era is the start of a new beginning!

I have put together some review questions for you to practice and remember to read this book over and over until you know that you have mastered the world of IP's.

IP is the core to networking!

I wish to thank everyone that have made this book possible and that includes you! May your quest for the CCNA certification come to fruition! For those that may be apprehensive about taking the certification exam…just think about this *"many before you have traveled that path and made it, so why shouldn't you*? No one is born a CCNA. Do you need to work hard at it? Most definitely! But anyone that focuses their minds to the task, are disciplined about their studies and have the passion to move forward, will always succeed. Just ask yourself this question – *"how bad do you want it?"*

Review Questions

1. What is the last valid host on the subnetwork
   172.18.31.96 255.255.255.240?
   a. 172.18.31.112
   b. 172.18.31.110
   c. 172.18.32.0
   d. 172.18.32.113

2. Which subnet does the host 172.17.44.142/28 belong to?
   a. 172.17.44.140
   b. 172.17.44.130
   c. 172.17.44.120
   d. 172.17.44.128

3. What valid host range is the IP address 172.17.101.106/23 a
   part of?
   a. 172.17.101.1 through to 172.17.101.255
   b. 172.17.10.1 through to 172.17.11.254
   c. 172.17.100.1 through to 172.17.101.254
   d. 172.17.100.0 through to 172.17.101.255

4. What is the first valid host on the subnetwork that the node
   172.18.96.246 255.255.254.0 belongs to?
   a. 172.18.96.1
   b. 172.18.96.221
   c. 172.18.96.11
   d. 172.18.96.245

5. What is the last valid host on the subnetwork
   192.168.226.128/26?
   a. 192.168.226.190
   b. 192.168.226.191
   c. 192.168.226.189
   d. 192.168.226.129

6. Which subnet does the host 10.87.179.200 255.255.240.0
   belong to?
   a. 10.87.144.0
   b. 10.87.176.0
   c. 10.87.178.0
   d. 10.87.160.0

7. What is the broadcast address of the network
   172.22.1.64 255.255.255.192?
   a. 172.22.1.128
   b. 172.22.1.126
   c. 172.22.1.127
   d. 172.22.1.255

8. What valid host range is the IP address
   172.22.48.115 255.255.255.128 a part of?
   a. 172.22.48.1 through to 172.22.48.126
   b. 172.22.48.0 through to 172.22.48.127
   c. 172.22.48.110 through to 172.22.48.128
   d. Invalid mask

9. You are designing a subnet mask for the 172.30.0.0 network. You want 600 subnets with up to 40 hosts on each subnet. What subnet mask should you use?

   a. 255.255.255.192

   b. 255.255.192.0

   c. 255.255.0.0

   d. 255.255.255.252

10. What is the broadcast address of the network 192.168.185.104/30?

    a. 192.168.185.105

    b. 192.168.185.106

    c. 192.168.185.107

    d. 192.168.185.108

11. Refer to the exhibit. The networks connected to router R2 have been summarized as a 192.168.176.0/21 route and sent to R1. Which two packet destination addresses will R1 forward to R2? (Choose two.)

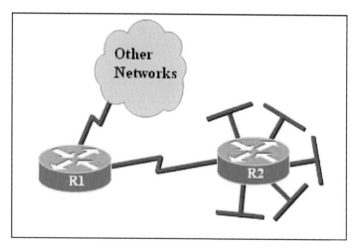

a. 192.168.194.160

b. 192.168.183.41

c. 192.168.159.2

d. 192.168.183.255

e. 192.168.179.4

f. 192.168.184.45

12. Refer to the exhibit. Which three statements correctly describe Network Device A?

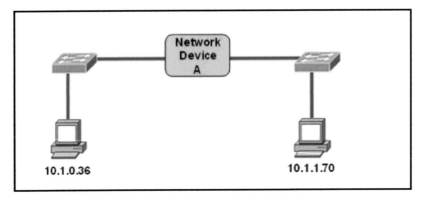

a. With a network wide mask of 255.255.255.128, each interface does not require an IP address.

b. With a network wide mask of 255.255.255.128, each interface does require an IP address on a unique IP subnet.

c. With a network wide mask of 255.255.255.0, must be a Layer 2 device for the PCs to communicate with each other.

d. With a network wide mask of 255.255.255.0, must be a Layer 3 device for the PCs to communicate with each other.

   e. With a network wide mask of 255.255.254.0, each interface does not require an IP address.

13. Which two statements describe characteristics of IPv6 unicast addressing? (Choose two.)

   a. Global addresses start with 2000::/3

   b. Link-local addresses start with FE00:/12

   c. Link-local addresses start with FF00::/10

   d. There is only one loopback address and it is ::1

   e. If a global address is assigned to an interface, then that is the only allowable address for the interface.

14. Which two of these statements are true of IPv6 address representation? (Choose two.)

   a. There are four types of IPv6 addresses: unicast, multicast, anycast, and broadcast.

   b. A single interface may be assigned multiple IPv6 addresses of any type.

   c. Every IPv6 interface contains at least one loopback address.

   d. The first 64 bits represent the dynamically created interface ID.

   e. Leading zeros in an IPv6 16 bit hexadecimal field are mandatory.

15. What is known as "one-to-nearest" addressing in IPv6?

   a. global unicast

   b. anycast

   c. multicast

d. unspecified address

16. Which option is a valid IPv6 address?
    a. 2001:0000:130F::099a::12a
    b. 2002:7654:A1AD:61:81AF:CCC1
    c. FEC0:ABCD:WXYZ:0067::2A4
    d. 2004:1:25A4:886F::1

17. How many bits are contained in each field of an IPv6 address?
    a. 24
    b. 4
    c. 8
    d. 16

18. Which IP address can be assigned to an Internet interface?
    a. 10.180.48.224
    b. 9.255.255.10
    c. 192.168.20.223
    d. 172.16.200.18

19. What will happen if a private IP address is assigned to a public interface connected to an ISP?
    a. Addresses in a private range will be not routed on the Internet backbone.
    b. Only the ISP router will have the capability to access the public network.
    c. The NAT process will be used to translate this address in a valid IP address.

d. Several automated methods will be necessary on the private network.

e. A conflict of IP addresses happens, because other public routers can use the same range.

20. Which term describes the process of encapsulating IPv6 packets inside IPv4 packets?

a. Tunneling

b. Hashing

c. Routing

d. NAT

21. Which statement about IPv6 is true?

a. Addresses are not hierarchical and are assigned at random.

b. Only one IPv6 address can exist on a given interface.

c. There are 2.7 billion addresses available.

d. Broadcasts have been eliminated and replaced with multicasts.

22. Refer to the exhibit. Which VLSM mask will allow for the appropriate number of host addresses for Network A?

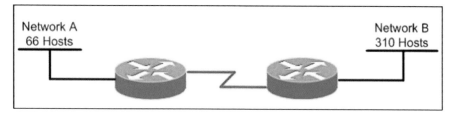

Network A
66 Hosts

Network B
310 Hosts

a. /25

b. /26

c. /27

    d. /28

23. Refer to the exhibit. Which subnet mask will place all hosts on Network B in the same subnet with the least amount of wasted addresses?

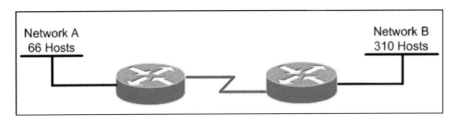

    a. 255.255.255.0

    b. 255.255.254.0

    c. 255.255.252.0

    d. 255.255.248.0

24. Refer to the exhibit. Which mask is correct to use for the WAN link between the routers that will provide connectivity while wasting the least amount of addresses?

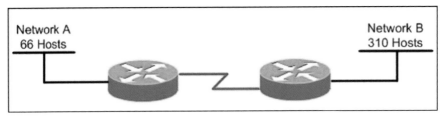

    a. /23

    b. /24

    c. /25

    d. /30

25. Refer to the exhibit. What is the most appropriate summarization for these routes?

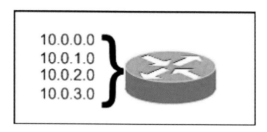

10.0.0.0
10.0.1.0
10.0.2.0
10.0.3.0

a. 10.0.0.0 /21
b. 10.0.0.0 /22
c. 10.0.0.0 /23
d. 10.0.0.0 /24

26. On the network 131.1.123.0/27, what is the last IP address that can be assigned to a host?
a. 131.1.123.30
b. 131.1.123.31
c. 131.1.123.32
d. 131.1.123.33

27. The ip subnet zero command is not configured on a router. What would be the IP address of Ethernet0/0 using the first available address from the sixth subnet of the network 192.168.8.0/29?
a. 192.168.8.25
b. 192.168.8.41
c. 192.168.8.49
d. 192.168.8.113

28. Which command would correctly configure a serial port on a router with the last usable host address in the 192.216.32.32/29 subnet?

    a. Router(config-if)# ip address 192.216.32.38
        255.255.255.240

    b. Router(config-if)# ip address 192.216.32.39
        255.255.255.224

    c. Router(config-if)# ip address 192.216.32.39
        255.255.255.224

    d. Router(config-if)# ip address 192.216.32.39
        255.255.255.248

    e. Router(config-if)# ip address 192.216.32.63
        255.255.255.248

    f. Router(config-if)# ip address 192.216.32.38
        255.255.255.248

29. The network default gateway applying to a host by DHCP is 192.168.5.33/28. Which option is the valid IP address of this host?

    a. 192.168.5.55

    b. 192.168.5.47

    c. 192.168.5.40

    d. 192.168.5.32

    e. 192.168.5.14

30. The network administrator has asked you to check the status of the workstation's IP stack by pinging the loopback address. Which address would you ping to perform this task?

    a. 10.1.1.1

    b. 127.0.0.1

    c. 192.168.0.1

    d. 239.1.1.1

31. Workstation A has been assigned an IP address of 192.0.2.24/28. Workstation B has been assigned an IP address of 192.0.2.100/28. The two workstations are connected with a straight-through cable. Attempts to ping between the hosts are unsuccessful. What two things can be done to allow communications between the hosts? (Choose two.)

    a. Replace the straight-through cable with a crossover cable.

    b. Change the subnet mask of the hosts to /25.

    c. Change the subnet mask of the hosts to /26.

    d. Change the address of Workstation A to 192.0.2.15.

    e. Change the address of Workstation B to 192.0.2.111.

32. Your ISP has given you the address 223.5.14.6/29 to assign to your router's interface. They have also given you the default gateway address of 223.5.14.7. After you have configured the address, the router is unable to ping any remote devices. What is preventing the router from pinging remote devices?

    a. The default gateway is not an address on this subnet.

    b. The default gateway is the broadcast address for this subnet.

    c. The IP address is the broadcast address for this subnet.

    d. The IP address is an invalid class D multicast address.

33. Refer to the exhibit. The user at Workstation B reports that Server A cannot be reached. What is preventing Workstation B from reaching Server A?

    a. The IP address for Server A is a broadcast address.

b. The IP address for Workstation B is a subnet address.

c. The gateway for Workstation B is not on the same subnet.

d. The gateway for Server A is not on the same subnet.

34. A national retail chain needs to design an IP addressing scheme to support a nationwide network. The company needs a minimum of 300 sub-networks and a maximum of 50 host addresses per subnet. Working with only one Class B address, which of the following subnet masks will support an appropriate addressing scheme? (Choose two.)

   a. 255.255.255.0

   b. 255.255.255.128

   c. 255.255.252.0

   d. 255.255.255.224

   e. 255.255.255.192

   f. 255.255.248.0

35. Refer to the diagram. All hosts have connectivity with one another. Which statements describe the addressing scheme that is in use in the network? (Choose three.)

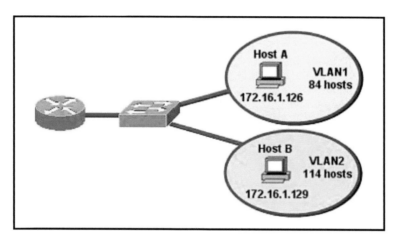

a. The subnet mask in use is 255.255.255.192.

b. The subnet mask in use is 255.255.255.128.

c. The IP address 172.16.1.25 can be assigned to hosts in VLAN1

d. The IP address 172.16.1.205 can be assigned to hosts in VLAN1

e. The LAN interface of the router is configured with one IP address.

f. The LAN interface of the router is configured with multiple IP addresses.

36. Refer to the exhibit. The network shown in the diagram is experiencing connectivity problems. Which of the following will correct the problems? (Choose two.)

a. Configure the gateway on Host A as 10.1.1.1.

b. Configure the gateway on Host B as 10.1.2.254

c. Configure the IP address of Host A as 10.1.2.2.

d. Configure the IP address of Host B as 10.1.2.2.

e. Configure the masks on both hosts to be 255.255.255.224.

f. Configure the masks on both hosts to be 255.255.255.240.

37. Which three IP addresses can be assigned to hosts if the subnet mask is /27 and subnet zero is usable? (Choose three.)
    a. 10.15.32.17
    b. 17.15.66.128
    c. 66.55.128.1
    d. 135.1.64.34
    e. 129.33.192.192
    f. 192.168.5.63

38. Running both IPv4 and IPv6 on a router simultaneously is known as what?
    a. 4to6 routing
    b. 6to4 routing
    c. binary routing
    d. dual-stack routing
    e. NextGen routing

39. What are three IPv6 transition mechanisms? (Choose three.)
    a. 6to4 tunneling
    b. VPN tunneling
    c. GRE tunneling
    d. ISATAP tunneling
    e. PPP tunneling
    f. Teredo tunneling

40. Identify the valid IPv6 addresses. (Choose all apply.)
    a. ::

    b. ::192:168:0:1

    c. 2000::

    d. 2001:3452:4952:2837::

    e. 2002:c0a8:101::42

    f. 2003:dead:beef:4dad:23:46:bb:101

41. Which of the following IP addresses can be assigned to the host devices? (Choose two.)

    a. 205.7.8.32/27

    b. 191.168.10.2/23

    c. 127.0.0.1

    d. 224.0.0.10

    e. 203.123.45.47/28

    f. 10.10.0.0/13

42. Refer to the exhibit. In this VLSM addressing scheme, what summary address would be sent from router A?

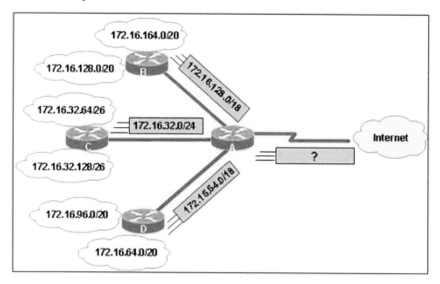

a. 172.16.0.0 /16

b. 172.16.0.0 /20

c. 172.16.0.0 /24

d. 172.32.0.0 /16

e. 172.32.0.0 /17

f. 172.64.0.0 /16

43. Which statement is true?

    a. An IPv6 address is 64 b long and is represented as hexadecimal characters.

    b. An IPv6 address is 32 b long and is represented as decimal digits.

    c. An IPv6 address is 128 b long and is represented as decimal digits. An IPv6 address is 128 b long and is represented as decimal digits.

    d. An IPv6 address is 128 b long and is represented as hexadecimal characters.

44. You are working in a data center environment and are assigned the address range 10.188.31.0/23.You are asked to develop an IP addressing plan to allow the maximum number of subnets with as many as 30 hosts each.Which IP address range meets these requirements?

    a. 10.188.31.0/27

    b. 10.188.31.0/26

    c. 10.188.31.0/29

    d. 10.188.31.0/28

    e. 10.188.31.0/25

45. Given an IP address 172.16.28.252 with a subnet mask of 255.255.240.0, what is the correct network addresss?

   a. 172.16.16.0

   b. 172.16.24.0

   c. 172.16.0.0

   d. 172.16.28.0

46. Which IPv6 address is valid?

   a. 2031:0:130F::9C0:876A:130B

   b. 2001:0DB8:0000:130F:0000:0000:08GC:140B

   c. 2001:0DB8:0:130H::87C:140B

   d. 2031::130F::9C0:876A:130B

47. Which command enables IPv6 forwarding on a cisco router?

   a. ipv6 host

   b. ipv6 unicast-routing

   c. ipv6 local

   d. ipv6 neighbor

48. What is the alternative notation for the IPV6 address B514:82C3:0000:0000:0029:EC7A:0000:EC72?

   a. B514:82C3:0029::EC7A:0000:EC72

   b. B514:82C3:0029:EC7A:EC72

   c. B514:82C3::0029:EC7A:0:EC72

   d. B514:82C3::0029:EC7A:EC72

49. Which IPV6 routing protocol uses multicast group FFO2::8 to send updates?

   a. RIPng
   b. OSPFv3
   c. IS-IS for IPv6
   d. Static

50. Wich command can you use to manually assign a static IPV6 address to a router interface?

   a. ipv6 address PREFIX_1::1/64
   b. ipv6 autoconfig 2001:db8:2222:7272::72/64
   c. ipv6 autoconfig
   d. ipv6 address 2001:db8:2222:7272::72/64

51. Which IPv6 routing protocol uses multicast group FF02::9 to send updates?

   a. RIPng
   b. OSPFv3
   c. Static
   d. IS-IS for IPv6

52. Which of these represents an IPv6 link-local address?

   a. FE08::280e:611:a:f14f:3d69
   b. FE81::280f:512b:e14f:3d69
   c. FE80::380e:611a:e14f:3d69
   d. FEFE:0345:5f1b::e14d:3d69

53. What are two features of the IPv6 protocol? (choose two)

a. complicated header

b. no broadcasts

c. checksums

d. IPsec Built in

e. Autoconfiguration

54. Which two are types of IPv6 addresses? (choose two)

a. Multicast

b. Broadcast

c. Allcast

d. Podcast

e. Anycast

55. The network administrator has been asked to give reasons for moving from IPv4 to IPv6. What are two valid reasons for adopting IPv6 over IPv4?(choose two)

a. telnet access does not require a password

b. nat

c. no broadcast

d. change of destination address in the IPv6 header

e. change of source address in the IPv6 header

f. autoconfiguration

56. Which address is a multicast group address that is used by RIPng as the destination address?

a. FF02::A

b. FF05::101

c. FF02::9

d. FF02::6

57. Which address is a multicast group address that is used by EIGRPv6 as the destination address?

    a. FF02::9
    b. FF02::10
    c. FF05::101
    d. FF02::A
    e. FF02::6

58. How many bits long is an IPv6 address?

    a. 32bits
    b. 64bits
    c. 128bits
    d. 255 bits

59. An IPv6 is broken up into two parts, what are those called?

    a. Network Prefix/Interface ID
    b. Subnet ID/Host ID
    c. OUI/ICU
    d. Left Side/Right Side

60. What is the purpose of using the EUI-64 command on a router?

    a. Enable routing
    b. Enable the RIPng and EIGRP protocol
    c. To auto configure the Interface ID using the MAC of the routers Interface
    d. To Statically assign an IP address on a routers interface

Workout Sheet

Workout Sheet

Answers to Review Questions

1. What is the last valid host on the subnetwork
   172.18.31.96 255.255.255.240?
   a. 172.18.31.112
   b. 172.18.31.110
   c. 172.18.32.0
   d. 172.18.32.113

2. Which subnet does the host 172.17.44.142/28 belong to?
   a. 172.17.44.140
   b. 172.17.44.130
   c. 172.17.44.120
   d. 172.17.44.128

3. What valid host range is the IP address 172.17.101.106/23 a
   part of?
   a. 172.17.101.1 through to 172.17.101.255
   b. 172.17.10.1 through to 172.17.11.254
   c. 172.17.100.1 through to 172.17.101.254
   d. 172.17.100.0 through to 172.17.101.255

4. What is the first valid host on the subnetwork that the node
   172.18.96.246 255.255.254.0 belongs to?
   a. 172.18.96.1
   b. 172.18.96.221
   c. 172.18.96.11
   d. 172.18.96.245

5. What is the last valid host on the subnetwork 192.168.226.128/26?

   a. 192.168.226.190

   b. 192.168.226.191

   c. 192.168.226.189

   d. 192.168.226.129

6. Which subnet does the host 10.87.179.200 255.255.240.0 belong to?

   a. 10.87.144.0

   b. 10.87.176.0

   c. 10.87.178.0

   d. 10.87.160.0

7. What is the broadcast address of the network 172.22.1.64 255.255.255.192?

   a. 172.22.1.128

   b. 172.22.1.126

   c. 172.22.1.127

   d. 172.22.1.255

8. What valid host range is the IP address 172.22.48.115 255.255.255.128 a part of?

   a. 172.22.48.1 through to 172.22.48.126

   b. 172.22.48.0 through to 172.22.48.127

   c. 172.22.48.110 through to 172.22.48.128

   d. Invalid mask

9. You are designing a subnet mask for the 172.30.0.0 network. You want 600 subnets with up to 40 hosts on each subnet. What subnet mask should you use?

   a. 255.255.255.192

   b. 255.255.192.0

   c. 255.255.0.0

   d. 255.255.255.252

10. What is the broadcast address of the network 192.168.185.104/30?

    a. 192.168.185.105

    b. 192.168.185.106

    c. 192.168.185.107

    d. 192.168.185.108

11. Refer to the exhibit. The networks connected to router R2 have been summarized as a 192.168.176.0/21 route and sent to R1. Which two packet destination addresses will R1 forward to R2? (Choose two.)

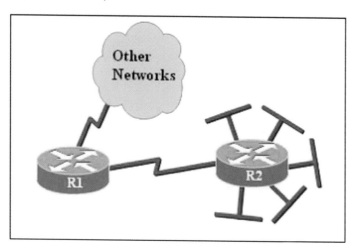

a. 192.168.194.160

b. 192.168.183.41

c. 192.168.159.2

d. 192.168.183.255

e. 192.168.179.4

f. 192.168.184.45

12. Refer to the exhibit. Which three statements correctly describe Network Device A?

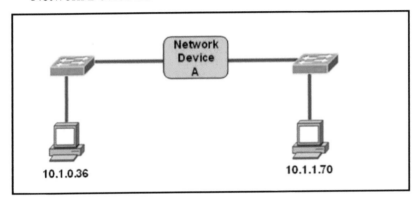

a. With a network wide mask of 255.255.255.128, each interface does not require an IP address.

b. With a network wide mask of 255.255.255.128, each interface does require an IP addresss on a unique IP subnet.

c. With a network wide mask of 255.255.255.0, must be a Layer 2 device for the PCs to communicate with each other.

d. With a network wide mask of 255.255.255.0, must be a Layer 3 device for the PCs to communicate with each other.

e. With a network wide mask of 255.255.254.0, each interface does not require an IP address.

13. Which two statements describe characteristics of IPv6 unicast addresssing? (Choose two.)

    a. Global addresses start with 2000::/3

    b. Link-local addresses start with FE00:/12

    c. Link-local addresses start with FF00::/10

    d. There is only one loopback address and it is ::1

    e. If a global address is assigned to an interface, then that is the only allowable addresses for the interface.

14. Which two of these statements are true of IPv6 address representation? (Choose two.)

    a. There are four types of IPv6 addresses: unicast, multicast, anycast, and broadcast.

    b. A single interface may be assigned multiple IPv6 addresses of any type.

    c. Every IPv6 interface contains at least one loopback address.

    d. The first 64 bits represent the dynamically created interface ID.

    e. Leading zeros in an IPv6 16 bit hexadecimal field are mandatory.

15. What is known as "one-to-nearest" addressing in IPv6?

    a. global unicast

    b. anycast

    c. multicast

    d. unspecified address

16. Which option is a valid IPv6 address?

    a. 2001:0000:130F::099a::12a

    b. 2002:7654:A1AD:61:81AF:CCC1

    c. FEC0:ABCD:WXYZ:0067::2A4

    d. 2004:1:25A4:886F::1

17. How many bits are contained in each field of an IPv6 address?

    a. 24

    b. 4

    c. 8

    d. 16

18. Which IP address can be assigned to an Internet interface?

    a. 10.180.48.224

    b. 9.255.255.10

    c. 192.168.20.223

    d. 172.16.200.18

19. What will happen if a private IP address is assigned to a public interface connected to an ISP?

    a. Addresses in a private range will be not routed on the Internet backbone.

    b. Only the ISP router will have the capability to access the public network.

    c. The NAT process will be used to translate this address in a valid IP addresss.

    d. Several automated methods will be necessary on the private network.

    e. A conflict of IP addresses happens, because other public routers can use the same range.

20. Which term describes the process of encapsulating IPv6 packets inside IPv4 packets?

    a. Tunneling

    b. Hashing

    c. Routing

    d. NAT

21. Which statement about IPv6 is true?

    a. Addresses are not hierarchical and are assigned at random.

    b. Only one IPv6 address can exist on a given interface.

    c. There are 2.7 billion addresses available.

    d. Broadcasts have been eliminated and replaced with multicasts.

22. Refer to the exhibit. Which VLSM mask will allow for the appropriate number of host addresses for Network A?

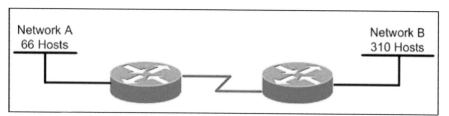

Network A
66 Hosts

Network B
310 Hosts

    a. /25

    b. /26

    c. /27

    d. /28

23. Refer to the exhibit. Which subnet mask will place all hosts on Network B in the same subnet with the least amount of wasted addresses?

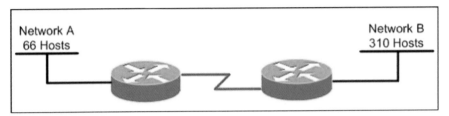

    a. 255.255.255.0

    b. 255.255.254.0

    c. 255.255.252.0

    d. 255.255.248.0

24. Refer to the exhibit. Which mask is correct to use for the WAN link between the routers that will provide connectivity while wasting the least amount of addresses?

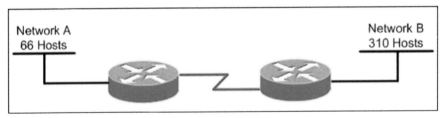

    a. /23

    b. /24

    c. /25

    d. /30

25. Refer to the exhibit. What is the most appropriate summarization for these routes?

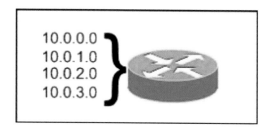

```
10.0.0.0
10.0.1.0
10.0.2.0
10.0.3.0
```

a. 10.0.0.0 /21

b. 10.0.0.0 /22

c. 10.0.0.0 /23

d. 10.0.0.0 /24

26. On the network 131.1.123.0/27, what is the last IP address that can be assigned to a host?

a. 131.1.123.30

b. 131.1.123.31

c. 131.1.123.32

d. 131.1.123.33

27. The ip subnet zero command is not configured on a router. What would be the IP address of Ethernet0/0 using the first available address from the sixth subnet of the network 192.168.8.0/29?

a. 192.168.8.25

b. 192.168.8.41

c. 192.168.8.49

d. 192.168.8.113

28. Which command would correctly configure a serial port on a router with the last usable host address in the 192.216.32.32/29 subnet?

a. Router(config-if)# ip address 192.216.32.38
255.255.255.240

b. Router(config-if)# ip address 192.216.32.39
255.255.255.224

c. Router(config-if)# ip address 192.216.32.39
255.255.255.224

d. Router(config-if)# ip address 192.216.32.39
255.255.255.248

e. Router(config-if)# ip address 192.216.32.63
255.255.255.248

f. Router(config-if)# ip address 192.216.32.38
255.255.255.248

29. The network default gateway applying to a host by DHCP is
192.168.5.33/28. Which option is the valid IP address of this
host?

a. 192.168.5.55

b. 192.168.5.47

c. 192.168.5.40

d. 192.168.5.32

e. 192.168.5.14

30. The network administrator has asked you to check the status of
the workstation's IP stack by pinging the loopback address.
Which address would you ping to perform this task?

a. 10.1.1.1

b. 127.0.0.1

c. 192.168.0.1

d. 239.1.1.1

31. Workstation A has been assigned an IP address of 192.0.2.24/28. Workstation B has been assigned an IP address of 192.0.2.100/28. The two workstations are connected with a straight-through cable. Attempts to ping between the hosts are unsuccessful. What two things can be done to allow communications between the hosts? (Choose two.)

    a. Replace the straight-through cable with a crossover cable.

    b. Change the subnet mask of the hosts to /25.

    c. Change the subnet mask of the hosts to /26.

    d. Change the address of Workstation A to 192.0.2.15.

    e. Change the address of Workstation B to 192.0.2.111.

32. Your ISP has given you the address 223.5.14.6/29 to assign to your router's interface. They have also given you the default gateway address of 223.5.14.7. After you have configured the address, the router is unable to ping any remote devices. What is preventing the router from pinging remote devices?

    a. The default gateway is not an address on this subnet.

    b. The default gateway is the broadcast address for this subnet.

    c. The IP address is the broadcast address for this subnet.

    d. The IP address is an invalid class D multicast address.

33. Refer to the exhibit. The user at Workstation B reports that Server A cannot be reached. What is preventing Workstation B from reaching Server A?

    a. The IP address for Server A is a broadcast address.

    b. The IP address for Workstation B is a subnet address.

    c. The gateway for Workstation B is not on the same subnet.

d. The gateway for Server A is not on the same subnet.

34. A national retail chain needs to design an IP addressing scheme to support a nationwide network. The company needs a minimum of 300 sub-networks and a maximum of 50 host addresses per subnet. Working with only one Class B address, which of the following subnet masks will support an appropriate addressing scheme? (Choose two.)

    a. 255.255.255.0
    b. 255.255.255.128
    c. 255.255.252.0
    d. 255.255.255.224
    e. 255.255.255.192
    f. 255.255.248.0

35. Refer to the diagram. All hosts have connectivity with one another. Which statements describe the addressing scheme that is in use in the network? (Choose three.)

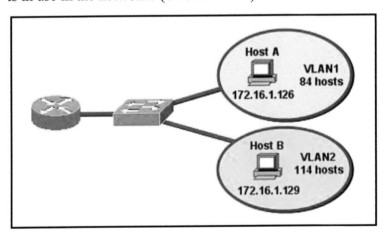

    a. The subnet mask in use is 255.255.255.192.
    b. The subnet mask in use is 255.255.255.128.

c. The IP address 172.16.1.25 can be assigned to hosts in VLAN1

d. The IP address 172.16.1.205 can be assigned to hosts in VLAN1

e. The LAN interface of the router is configured with one IP address.

f. The LAN interface of the router is configured with multiple IP addresses.

36. Refer to the exhibit. The network shown in the diagram is experiencing connectivity problems. Which of the following will correct the problems? (Choose two.)

a. Configure the gateway on Host A as 10.1.1.1.

b. Configure the gateway on Host B as 10.1.2.254

c. Configure the IP address of Host A as 10.1.2.2.

d. Configure the IP address of Host B as 10.1.2.2.

e. Configure the masks on both hosts to be 255.255.255.224.

f. Configure the masks on both hosts to be 255.255.255.240.

37. Which three IP addresses can be assigned to hosts if the subnet mask is /27 and subnet zero is usable? (Choose three.)

a. 10.15.32.17

b. 17.15.66.128

c. 66.55.128.1

d. 135.1.64.34

e. 129.33.192.192

f. 192.168.5.63

38. Running both IPv4 and IPv6 on a router simultaneously is known as what?

a. 4to6 routing

b. 6to4 routing

c. binary routing

d. dual-stack routing

e. NextGen routing

39. What are three IPv6 transition mechanisms? (Choose three.)

a. 6to4 tunneling

b. VPN tunneling

c. GRE tunneling

d. ISATAP tunneling

e. PPP tunneling

f. Teredo tunneling

40. Identify the valid IPv6 addresses. (Choose all apply.)

a. ::

b. ::192:168:0:1

c. 2000::

d. 2001:3452:4952:2837::

e. 2002:c0a8:101::42

f. 2003:dead:beef:4dad:23:46:bb:101

41. Which of the following IP addresses can be assigned to the host devices? (Choose two.)

a. 205.7.8.32/27

b. 191.168.10.2/23

c. 127.0.0.1

d. 224.0.0.10

e. 203.123.45.47/28

f. 10.10.0.0/13

42. Refer to the exhibit. In this VLSM addressing scheme, what summary address would be sent from router A?

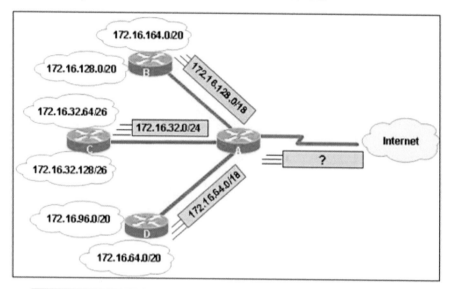

a. 172.16.0.0 /16

b. 172.16.0.0 /20

c. 172.16.0.0 /24

d. 172.32.0.0 /16

e. 172.32.0.0 /17

f. 172.64.0.0 /16

43. Which statement is true?

a. An IPv6 address is 64 b long and is represented as hexadecimal characters.

b. An IPv6 address is 32 b long and is represented as decimal digits.

c. An IPv6 address is 128 b long and is represented as decimal digits. An IPv6 address is 128 b long and is represented as decimal digits.

d. An IPv6 address is 128 b long and is represented as hexadecimal characters.

44. You are working in a data center environment and are assigned the address range 10.188.31.0/23.You are asked to develop an IP addressing plan to allow the maximum number of subnets with as many as 30 hosts each.Which IP address range meets these requirements?

a. 10.188.31.0/27

b. 10.188.31.0/26

c. 10.188.31.0/29

d. 10.188.31.0/28

e. 10.188.31.0/25

45. Given an IP address 172.16.28.252 with a subnet mask of 255.255.240.0, what is the correct network addresss?

a. 172.16.16.0

b. 172.16.24.0

c. 172.16.0.0

d. 172.16.28.0

46. Which IPv6 address is valid?

a. 2031:0:130F::9C0:876A:130B

b. 2001:0DB8:0000:130F:0000:0000:08GC:140B

c. 2001:0DB8:0:130H::87C:140B

d. 2031::130F::9C0:876A:130B

47. Which command enables IPv6 forwarding on a cisco router?

    a. ipv6 host

    b. ipv6 unicast-routing

    c. ipv6 local

    d. ipv6 neighbor

48. What is the alternative notation for the IPV6 address B514:82C3:0000:0000:0029:EC7A:0000:EC72?

    a. B514:82C3:0029::EC7A:0000:EC72

    b. B514:82C3:0029:EC7A:EC72

    c. B514:82C3::0029:EC7A:0:EC72

    d. B514:82C3::0029:EC7A:EC72

49. Which IPV6 routing protocol uses multicast group FFO2::8 to send updates?

    a. RIPng

    b. OSPFv3

    c. IS-IS for IPv6

    d. Static

50. Wich command can you use to manually assign a static IPV6 address to a router interface?

    a. ipv6 address PREFIX_1::1/64

    b. ipv6 autoconfig 2001:db8:2222:7272::72/64

    c. ipv6 autoconfig

    d. ipv6 address 2001:db8:2222:7272::72/64

51. Which IPv6 routing protocol uses multicast group FF02::9 to send updates?

    a. RIPng
    b. OSPFv3
    c. Static
    d. IS-IS for IPv6

52. Which of these represents an IPv6 link-local address?

    a. FE08::280e:611:a:f14f:3d69
    b. FE81::280f:512b:e14f:3d69
    c. FE80::380e:611a:e14f:3d69
    d. FEFE:0345:5f1b::e14d:3d69

53. What are two features of the IPv6 protocol? (choose two)

    a. complicated header
    b. no broadcasts
    c. checksums
    d. IPsec Built in
    e. Autoconfiguration

54. Which two are types of IPv6 addresses? (choose two)

    a. Multicast
    b. Broadcast
    c. Allcast
    d. Podcast
    e. Anycast

55. The network administrator has been asked to give reasons for moving from IPv4 to IPv6. What are two valid reasons for adopting IPv6 over IPv4?(choose two)

a. telnet access does not require a password

b. nat

c. no broadcast

d. change of destination address in the IPv6 header

e. change of source address in the IPv6 header

f. autoconfiguration

56. Which address is a multicast group address that is used by RIPng as the destination address?

a. FF02::A

b. FF05::101

c. FF02::9

d. FF02::6

57. Which address is a multicast group address that is used by EIGRPv6 as the destination address?

a. FF02::9

b. FF02::10

c. FF05::101

d. FF02::A

e. FF02::6

58. How many bits long is an IPv6 address?

a. 32bits

b. 64bits

c. 128bits

d. 255 bits

59. An IPv6 is broken up into two parts, what are those called?
    a. Network Prefix/Interface ID
    b. Subnet ID/Host ID
    c. OUI/ICU
    d. Left Side/Right Side

60. What is the purpose of using the EUI-64 command on a router?
    a. Enable routing
    b. Enable the RIPng and EIGRP protocol
    c. To auto configure the Interface ID using the MAC of the routers Interface
    d. To Statically assign an IP address on a routers interface

Special Thanks

I would also like to thank the following people for their collaboration in helping me with putting this book together. Without their creativity in the design, formatting & editing, I would not be able to provide you with such a wonderful finished product and one that I am very proud of. – Not bad for being my first Book!

(1) Natalia from Croatia & her company *"Book Design Team"* in the editing and formatting of this book to get it ready for publishing. *"Thanks for your professional and timely work!"*

(2) The awesome book cover was created by a person that would like to remain anonymous. *"Thank you for an awesome job! It's exactly how I imagined it".*

(3) Mary Wiekel, from the US & her company *"Pinkblooddesigns"* in formatting the book cover to comply with the publisher's standards. *"Great work!"*

About the Author

Lazaro J Diaz, better known as "Laz", was born in Cuba and fled the communist country with his family to the United States in 1973, when he was only 6 years old. He graduated from Miami High in 1985 and continued on to join the military in 1986.

He has a daughter, Cynthia from his first marriage and met his current wife in 1999. At that time he was forced to go to school and start his career as a Network Engineer. His previous jobs where in warehousing & construction. Please note that before starting his career in IT, Laz had never touched a computer and thought that YAHOO was a word used by cowboys.

Laz graduated from Florida Career College with honors and was the speaker at his graduation ceremony. This same school later hired him to teach and he held on to this position for over 8 years before resigning. He received "Faculty of the Year" awards for 3 consecutive years and other recognitions from this institution.

Before his graduation and after his resignation at FCC, he also taught at various educational institutions (i.e.: Palm Beach Community College, New Horizons & The Academy of South Florida), teaching both Cisco, Microsoft and other IT certification preparation courses in Miami, Florida – USA.

Laz has over 13 years in the teaching industry and in the field working with telecommunications and cellular companies. He is best known for his unique style of teaching and his very own, but unconventional, method of conveying the information. This is his trademark and is what has made him popular amongst those that are looking for a different type of instructor that can convey the information in a simplistic manner.

He has his own training center where students go to get hands on practice and receive their CCNA certification preparation from Laz himself.

Laz has published several online video tutorial courses for the CCNA certification exam and is well known to his students as a person that cares and is passionate about teaching. He has reached and taught thousands of students worldwide with his tutorials, onsite and online training center to include corporate clients and IT professionals.

Laz believes that the only way anyone can break-free of oppression and be able to provide a better future for themselves and their family is through education. That is why he has made it his mission to be able to provide education that is affordable, and to some, even free.

His YouTube channel started as a prank with his now infamous "IP addressing and Subnetting" video. This was filmed at his home by his wife Digna, with a hand-held, non-HD camera, no lighting and no professional audio. This was the beginning of an online teaching career that has now transpired into other mediums to include this book.

Laz plans on writing other books in the near future that will be geared towards other areas within Cisco. This one, however, is the very first book he has authored!

Laz lives in Miami, Florida, with his wife, Digna, and is now producing his very own internet TV channel called *"Live with Laz – Cisco Training"* to give everyone an opportunity to receive an affordable education.

IP BOOK

LINKS

www.thenetworkingdoctors.com

www.udemy.com/u/infothenetworkingdoctorscom

www.on-ed.com

www.wiziq.com/cisco

www.cisco.patience.io

www.youtube.com/TheNetworkingDoctors

www.twitter.com/networkingdrs

www.linkedin/in/thenetworkingdoctors

U.S. Copyright © 2014

Color Version

ISBN-13: 978-1499745221

ISBN-10: 1499745222

CPSIA information can be obtained at www.ICGtesting.com
Printed in the USA
LVIW01n2300040117
519789LV00004B/6